Stress Management for Teacher

Also available from Continuum:

Helping Young People to Beat Stress, Sarah McNamara

How to Manage Stress in FE, Elizabeth Hartney

Stress Busting, Michael Papworth

Stress Management for Teachers

ELIZABETH HARTNEY

continuum

Continuum International Publishing Group

The Tower Building   80 Maiden Lane
11 York Road   Suite 704
London   New York
SE1 7NX   NY 10038

www.continuumbooks.com

British Library Cataloguing-in-Publication Data
A catalogue record for this book is available from the British Library.

ISBN: 9–7808–2649–6072 (paperback)

Library of Congress Cataloging-in-Publication Data
A catalog record for this book is available from the Library of Congress.

Typeset by BookEns Ltd, Royston, Herts.
Printed and bound in Great Britain by Cromwell Press, Wilshire

For Jason

Contents

Introduction   1

Chapter 1: Why we need stress management

Definitions of stress   6
Stress in teachers   7
What is the point of stress management?   8
What stress can do to your physical health   9
What stress can do to your mental health   11
What stress can do to your quality of life   12
How stress can affect your career   14

Chapter 2: Understanding stress

Performance and stress   16
Positive and negative stress   18
Stress, motivation and change   19
How to know when you are under too much stress   20
What to do if you are under too much stress   23
Managing the symptoms of stress in teaching   24
Managing the causes of stress in teaching   39

Chapter 3: Stress in teaching

The process of teaching   50
Your identity as a teacher   53
The politics of teaching   56

Chapter 4: Career development

The 'professional' teacher   62
The 'manager-in-training'   63
The 'fall-back' teacher   65
The 'day-job' teacher   66
The 'undefined career' teacher   67
Self-reflection: what kind of teacher are you?   69
Our personal career goals: a source of stress   69

Chapter 5: Relationships at work

Introduction   74
Reciprocity   74
Relationship rules   77
Power plays   81
Bullying   84

Chapter 6: Dealing with difficult people

Personalities versus behaviours   90
Behaviours and styles of communication   90
Communication scenario   92
Difficult personality styles   94
Are you a difficult person?   101

Chapter 7: Balancing professional and personal life

Why you should value your home life   104
How personal relationships are different from
    professional relationships   104
Boundaries in personal relationships   105
Family relationships   107
New relationships   107

Marriage   108
Pregnancy, childbirth and childcare   109
Divorce   111
Bereavement   112
Coping with family problems   112
Friendships   113
Community   114

Chapter 8: Managing feelings

Understanding emotion   116
When you feel angry   117
When you feel scared   119
When you feel sad or hurt   120
When you need help coping with your feelings   122

Chapter 9: Managing your health

Chronic and acute health problems   129
Recognize the warning signs   131
Cigarettes, alcohol and drugs   133
Enjoying taking care of yourself   135
Getting treatment   135

Chapter 10: Stress management for life

Putting it all together   139
Projecting a professional image   140
Summary of previous chapters   142
Summary of techniques   144
Conclusion   147

Further resources

Teaching-specific resources	149
Helplines	151
Websites	152
Audio/video/DVD	154
Image and dress	154
References	156
Index	170

This book presents a basic understanding of stress, in the context of teaching, and the effects of stress on personal and professional well-being. It also provides strategies for managing the many stressors that affect teachers, from career planning to dealing with difficult people. Over the past few decades there have been many changes in circumstances that affect teachers, and the job has become more and more stressful. However, at the time of writing, exciting changes are afoot to alleviate many of the stressors teachers have endured, and the implications of these changes are incorporated into the advice contained in this book.

Chapter 1 covers the rationale for the book. It begins with definitions of stress in the academic literature, and then addresses the findings of research on stress in teachers as a specific occupational group. It continues by justifying the importance of teachers using stress management, based on research demonstrating the dangers of stress to physical and mental health, and its detrimental effects on quality of life and career progression.

Chapter 2 is concerned with providing an understanding of what stress is. It outlines the relationship between performance and stress, and the positive as well as negative aspects of moderate stress, including stress as a source of motivation, stress as a focus for achieving targets and stress as a source of energy. Chapter 2 also includes a brief questionnaire for readers to test whether or not they are under too much stress, and offers suggestions for what to do if you are.

Chapter 3 addresses stress in teaching specifically. A review of the literature on stress in teachers forms the basis for this chapter. Three major areas of stress that affect teachers are identified: stress during teaching itself, stress resulting from your self-image as a teacher and stress resulting from the politics of teaching. Tips for dealing with each of these sources of stress are presented.

Chapter 4 looks at career development in education. Readers are encouraged to reflect on their motivations for teaching, and personal career goals are identified as a source of stress in themselves. Building on arguments made in previous chapters, Chapter 4 goes on to focus on directing energy towards goal achievement, the often stressful task of self-promotion and the failure versus feedback approach to coping with disappointment.

Chapter 5 deals with a universal source of stress, that of relationships at work. Literature regarding the importance of reciprocity in relationships and abiding by relationship rules is presented in the context of the educational environment. Chapter 5 also addresses situations where others do not always play by the rules, and offers suggestions for dealing with power plays and bullying.

Chapter 6 focuses on dealing with difficult people. The distinction is made between people's personalities and their behaviours. Aggressive, assertive, passive and indirect behaviours are identified and illustrated with examples. Four personality types commonly described as difficult to deal with are then identified: bossy people, manipulative people, moody people and lazy people. The pitfalls of working with each of the difficult personality types are identified, along with strategies for handling them. Finally, brief advice is offered for readers who identify themselves as difficult people.

Chapter 7 discusses the challenges of balancing professional and personal life. After clarifying the importance of personal relationships, differences between personal and professional relationships are identified. Stresses related to a range of personal life situations, including new relationships, marriage, pregnancy, childbirth, childcare, divorce and bereavement are addressed, along with advice and ideas of where to seek further help.

Chapter 8 is concerned with managing feelings. The chapter begins with a short section on understanding emotion, followed by dedicated sections on managing anger, fear and sadness. The remainder of Chapter 8 is focused on the different approaches to coping with feelings including counselling and psychotherapy, coaching and mentoring, self-help groups, helplines and self-help books.

Chapter 9 looks at managing your health. After making the distinction between chronic and acute health problems, information is given to help readers to recognize the warning signs of stress affecting their health. It goes on to detail health-promoting habits, which counteract the effects of stress, and to encourage readers to enjoy taking care of themselves. Finally, advice is given on obtaining appropriate treatment, including complementary therapies.

The final chapter rounds up information provided throughout the book. This includes advice on integrating the various pieces of advice and information, along with suggestions on projecting a professional image. Previous chapters and techniques addressed throughout the book are summarized, along with the conclusion.

Disclaimer

This book is intended to help teachers to cope with everyday stress in the normal course of their duties. It is not intended as a substitute for medical or therapeutic attention, including the diagnosis of mental or physical health problems. Neither is it intended as a substitute for taking appropriate action in the case of harassment, abuse or other unacceptable work-related situations. Readers are encouraged to discuss any lifestyle changes suggested here with their doctors, particularly in the case of dietary change and exercise. The author cannot be held responsible for any consequences arising from the advice presented in this book.

1

WHY WE NEED STRESS MANAGEMENT

Definitions of stress

The first step in understanding why stress management is important is in understanding what stress actually is. We hear the term 'stress' on a daily basis, yet people's views on stress vary greatly. What is considered stressful to one person may not be considered stressful at all to someone else.

Stress has entered the popular vocabulary and is generally understood as a physical, mental or emotional reaction to unpleasant circumstances. It can be used to describe external problems, such as 'stress at work', an internal feeling of being 'stressed out', or pressure, which may even improve performance (Jones & Bright, 2001). This book will address all three types of stress by looking at ways to respond appropriately to external problems associated with working in teaching, to understand the internal feelings which are a consequence and to make use of stress to get the most out of your career.

Early definitions of stress were concerned with the effects of threats on the body. Stress was seen as a state of stimulation causing the 'fight or flight' response, a higher level of physical arousal to escape or fight off the threat (Cannon, 1932), and to cope with 'stressors' (events that cause stress) through an alarm reaction (Selye, 1956). These physical reactions were considered to be important in allowing us to adapt and survive in difficult circumstances. Even these early theories recognized that stress involves a physical response and can have detrimental effects on the body over time. More recent research has shown that stress is indeed implicated in a wide range of physical and mental complaints, underlining the importance of learning and practising effective stress management techniques, which are available to everyone. This book will address some of the physical consequences of long-term stress and its effects on our physical, mental and emotional health. It also recognizes that illness, whether caused by stress or not, is a cause of stress in itself, and one which must be carefully responded to in order to continue to get the most out of working in teaching.

Later definitions of stress emphasized the context and situations in which stress occurs, focusing on issues such as life events (Holmes & Rahe, 1967). These will be discussed in more detail in Chapter 7. More recently, Lazarus and Folkman (1984) developed the idea that stress does not simply happen automatically, but that you go through a complex series of 'appraisals' or judgements of the stress-inducing situation, which affect how 'stressed out' you actually become. It is this process of appraisal that allows you to respond to stress in different ways, including the stress-management strategies described in this book.

Stress in teachers

Stress among teachers is well recognized, both in the research literature (Kyriacou, 2001) and in mainstream society. The stress that is inherent in teaching appears to be universal across nations and cultures, with studies from around the world documenting stress in teachers in locations as varied as China (Wang & Guo, 2007), Hong Kong (Hui & Chan, 1996), Singapore (Ko et al., 2000), South Africa (Van der Lindl, 2001), the Middle East (Al-Mohannadi & Capel, 2007), Australia (Hart et al., 1995), the USA (Yoon, 2002), Canada (Chorney, 1998), Germany (Klusmann et al., 2006), the Netherlands (Van Horn et al., 2001), Finland (Ritvanen et al., 2006), Sweden (Jacobsson et al., 2001), Greece (Antoniou et al., 2006) and the UK (PricewaterhouseCoopers, 2001). UK teachers fare particularly badly, with greater levels of stress and stress-related indicators than other European countries (Griva & Joekes, 2003), although a cross-cultural study of teachers in Australia and Scotland showed stress levels to be similar (Pithers & Soden, 1998).

Stories of teachers being stressed to the limits abound, with newspaper reports and television programmes frequently detailing the struggles teachers endure. Despite the negative focus of much high-profile media, which may have inadvertently contributed to both the public and private perception of teachers as being unable to cope, it has undoubtedly contributed to greater public recognition of the extreme stress teachers have been subjected to in recent years. This has finally lead to the

7

beginnings of positive change in factors affecting teachers on a political level, which is only now beginning to translate into legislation and policies that have the potential to alleviate some aspects of teacher stress. The implications of these changes will be explored in greater detail later in the book.

Despite the recognition of some of the bureaucratic aspects of teacher stress, and measures to address it, teachers have to cope with a challenging and potentially stressful job day-to-day in a society that often portrays teaching in a less than favourable light. This book is intended to challenge the view that teaching has to be plagued by these negative perceptions. Its aim is to empower you, to recognize your own successes as a teacher and to respect the important professional role you fulfil, for the individual children you work with, for the contribution you make to society and for the immeasurable impact you have on the future development of the human race. By respecting and valuing the contribution you make, as a member of 'the noblest profession', you can begin to change your expectations about how you are treated by others, both in and out of school.

Some sources of stress for teachers are not directly related to the work involved in teaching and are beyond the control of the individual teacher, for example job security, resources and political issues in education. Although these stressors have a direct impact on teachers, and more changes are certainly needed on a societal level to reduce the stress on teachers, the focus of this book will be on how individual teachers respond to these stressors, rather than how change should occur on an organizational or political level.

What is the point of stress management?

At first glance, stress management might appear to be a waste of time. Often when working with clients on stress management, I find that their response is: '*I am already stressed! Stress management just gives me more to worry about and more to do!*' Well, in some ways that is true. In order for stress management to work, there is an initial outlay in terms of time, thought, planning and taking action. Reading this book is one example of an activity that takes time and thought. However, the benefits of stress management are that by becoming aware of ways in which you are unnecessarily causing yourself more stress, you can learn ways that your overall stress levels can be reduced. Positive effects include better health, better relationships and a better quality of life. People who follow through with stress management typically find that it is effective and well worth the effort.

This view is supported by research. Many studies evaluating the effectiveness of stress management strategies show that the development of relaxation skills (Reynolds et al., 1993; Heron et al., 1999; Teasdale et al., 2000), time management (Reynolds et al., 1993) and exercise (Whatmore et al., 1999) assisted individuals with workplace stress. These are covered in more detail in Chapter 2.

As all of the above skills can be self-taught, you can benefit greatly from using self-help books such as this one; CDs, tapes, DVDs or downloads that teach relaxation, time management and exercise; and participation in workshops, classes and self-help groups. Workshops, classes and self-help groups give the added social support of a group, which has been shown to help teachers to cope with stress (Sheffield et al., 1994). More details of how to develop these skills can be found in Chapter 2.

What stress can do to your physical health

Even the earliest theories of stress recognized that it could have a negative effect on the body. There has been a great deal of research showing the various ways that stress can take its toll on your physical health. Table 1 summarizes research studies that show some of the ways that stress can cause physical damage. Details on where the full research reports can be found are in the References at the end of the book. For more information on the various ways that stress can cause disease, see Sapolsky (2004), which provides a detailed, readable and humorous account of the physiology of stress, along with issues related to coping.

Table 1: How stress can damage your physical health

Health problem	Research showing impact of stress
Common cold	Cohen, Tyrrell & Smith (1991)
Slower wound healing	Kiecolt-Glaser & Glaser (1995) Marucha, Kiecolt-Glaser & Favagehi (1998)
Hypertension	Cobb & Rose (1973)
Coronary heart disease	Karasek, Baker, Marxer, Ahlbom & Theorell (1981)
	Lynch, Krause, Kaplan, Tuomilehto & Salonen (1997)
	Kivimäki, Leino-Arjas, Luukkonen, Riihimäki, Vahtera & Kirjonen (2002)
Cancer	Laudenslager, Ryan, Drugan, Hyson & Maier (1983)
HIV disease progression	Solomon, Temoshok, O'Leary & Zich (1987)
	Reed, Kemeny, Taylor & Visscher (1999)

Stress affects your health in many different ways – some direct, some indirect. One of the ways that stress affects your health most directly is by reducing the effectiveness of the immune system, the body's means of fighting disease. More indirect ways that stress can affect your health relate to your behaviour. As a result of stress you are more likely to engage in unhealthy behaviours such as smoking or drinking alcohol and caffeine, which cause you even more stress in the long run. Furthermore, you are less likely to engage in activities that would protect your health, such as eating a healthy diet (Baucom & Aiken, 1981; Conner et al., 1999), taking regular exercise (Metcalfe et al., 2003) and sleeping well. Finally, when you are under stress, you are more likely to have accidents (Lusa et al., 2002).

What stress can do to your mental health

Stress has been implicated in depression (Jones & Bright, 2001; Karasek, 1990), and a sense of control over your job lowers the incidence of a wide range of symptoms, including depression, exhaustion, heart problems, dizziness and headaches (Karasek, 1990; also see Sapolsky (2004) for physiological details of how stress can affect your mental health and cognitive processes). It is well known that stress at work can lead to the development of 'burnout'. Although burnout is slightly different from depression, there is a connection between the two, and Bakker et al.'s (2000) research found that burnout in teachers leads to depression.

Although the term 'burnout' is used in everyday language to refer to a wide range of job-related issues, when researchers refer to burnout it relates specifically to the symptoms detailed below (Maslach et al., 2001; Taris et al., 2004). Burnout is a condition that primarily affects people who work in roles supporting others, and teachers are prone to burnout because of their relationships with large numbers of students, staff and administrators (Blix et al., 1994). For this reason, there are several chapters in this book that are devoted to reducing the stress caused by these working relationships.

What is burnout?

Burnout consists of three central components:

- *Emotional exhaustion*: This involves the depletion of energy or draining of our emotional resources. The comment: *'I have no energy for a life outside of work'* might be made by someone suffering from emotional exhaustion.
- *Depersonalization*: This involves psychological withdrawal from relationships with our students and/or colleagues, and the development of negative, cynical attitudes towards others. Comments like: *'My students are all lazy and are not interested in learning what I have to teach them'* indicates someone is suffering from depersonalization.

- *Lack of personal accomplishment*: This is the tendency to make negative judgements of our own competence and achievement in our work, along with feelings of insufficiency and low self-esteem. A teacher who says: '*None of the students understood anything in that last class. Maybe I just don't have what it takes*' might be suffering from lack of personal accomplishment.

How burnout affects teachers will be explored in more detail in Chapter 3.

In summary, the literature indicates that teachers universally experience a high level of stress at work. Stressors relate to difficulties with work relationships (including relationships with large numbers of students and colleagues), which may range from subtle communication difficulties to bullying and harassment (addressed in detail in later chapters), and may result in poor health and burnout. The National Union of Teachers (NUT) believe that the problem of stress in schools is underestimated, and that more than half of retirements for ill-health in recent years have been stress related (National Union of Teachers, 1999).

What stress can do to your quality of life

Stress at work can impact not only your quality of life at work but can also 'spill over' into your home life, affecting your relationships, your well-being and your happiness. Although motivations to work are complex and may be largely financial (discussed further in Chapter 4), long-term stress impacting upon your happiness can lead to a quality of life that is seriously detrimental to you as an individual. A sense of helplessness and hopelessness about the situation, without the recognition that change is possible, can in some cases lead to years of unnecessary unhappiness.

A poor quality of life may involve the experience of burnout, in which you feel exhausted, you cease to feel invested in the work that you do and you disconnect from relationships with others. It may involve either emotional or physical exhaustion, or both. When your sleep patterns are affected by stress, the sense of exhaustion can become a way of life. Something as simple as learning to manage stress so that you can develop good sleep patterns can turn this around very quickly, and revitalize your experience of life.

It is increasingly common for people to see self-medication as a solution to physical and emotional problems. This may involve taking sleep medication, which is addictive and rarely leads to restful sleep. Alternatively, alcohol intake may be increased in an attempt to relax (Hartney et al., 2003), cigarettes may be used for both stimulation and relaxation (although they are rarely effective in either capacity in the long term) and caffeine may be used for stimulation (again, rarely effective due to the dependency caused, which leads to a greater level of tiredness). Furthermore, nicotine, caffeine and alcohol can all interfere with normal sleep patterns, and dealing with toxins puts the body under greater strain. A US study of drug use in teachers showed that teachers use significantly more alcohol, amphetamines and tranquillizers than a national sample, and that drug use in teachers is related to stress (Watts & Short, 1990).

Long-term stress can also affect your self-image, actually making you define yourself in terms of how much stress you are under. Despite this, you may not take responsibility for making changes ('victim mode'), or you may feel you should be able to withstand unlimited stress ('invincible mode'). When I was working in stress management, I used to see both of these patterns of self-image with great frequency.

The biggest problem resulting from having a self-image that is tied up with stress is that it makes it more difficult for you to change, because any change becomes a threat to your identity. When you get stuck in 'victim mode' you tend to relate to others by complaining about how much stress you are under. In order to change, you have to develop a new self-image, one of being able to take responsibility for competently managing your own stress. If you get stuck in 'invincible mode' you feel robbed of your identity when your body eventually cannot take the strain any more, leaving you fatigued and unwell. This can even lead to chronic pain. In order to learn how to manage stress, you first have to accept you are as weak as everyone else.

Conversely, recognizing the potential that stress has to rob you of years of your life, which could be happy and fulfilling, is important in starting to implement the stress-management strategies in this book. Once you recognize that change is possible, and that both your experiences and your perceptions of stress can be radically different, you begin to take control of your life, and thereby improve your quality of life.

How stress can affect your career

Stress can have a variety of effects on your experience of work. Some people seem to thrive in a stressful environment (this is discussed further in Chapter 2), while others develop burnout (see pages 11–12) very quickly in stressful circumstances. Experimental research has shown that higher work demands lead to both greater arousal (alertness) and poorer performance (Parkes et al., 1990). Higher task demands have also been shown to produce more negative moods and, although more may be accomplished, more mistakes are made (Searle et al., 1999). Interestingly, although the factors that cause stress impair task performance, there is no relationship between people's *experience* of stress and their task performance, meaning that, although the high demands that cause poor performance also cause stress, stress itself does not necessarily affect performance in experimental conditions (Jones & Bright, 2001). The complex relationship between stress and performance is discussed in more detail in Chapter 2.

There are also longer-term effects that stress can have on your career. When you are burnt out you can find yourself either obsessed with work or stuck in a rut. Either way, you can end up in a job you do not enjoy.

2

Understanding
Stress

Performance and stress

Have you ever wondered why some people thrive on stress and never seem to get ill, while others crumble under the slightest pressure? The ways that stress affects us are complex and are due to many factors, which will be considered in this chapter.

The presence of stressors does not inevitably lead to us experiencing stress. According to the transactional view of stress (Lazarus & Folkman, 1984), it is the way that a potentially stressful situation is evaluated and responded to that determines whether it will have an effect, and whether that effect will be positive or negative.

Whether stress will negatively affect your performance also depends on your 'hardiness'. Hardiness is a combination of commitment, control and challenge, which counteract the negative effects of stress by influencing the way you feel, think and act during the experience of work stress (Kobasa, 1979). Research shows that people with higher levels of hardiness report fewer hassles and stressful life events, and also judge those hassles that are experienced to be less severe than people who have lower levels of hardiness (Banks & Gannon, 1988). Hardy people do not experience fewer stressful events, but simply seem to perceive them as less stressful. That is, they 'appraise' events as less stressful. Research shows that in exactly the same situation, hardy people experience lower stress levels than less hardy people. Hardy people seem to assess their ability more highly, resulting in lower stress (Westman, 1990). Furthermore, they tend to have a more optimistic attitude towards coping with stress, by focusing on positive aspects of the situation and confronting rather than ignoring their problems.

The strategies in this book are designed to encourage and develop a 'hardy' approach to dealing with stress in teaching, by recognizing and dealing with the causes of stress that affect teachers, and recognizing the positive aspects of the choices you make that are related to your work.

Gmelch (1983) argued that too little stress, described as 'rustout', is as damaging as too much stress, or 'burnout'. When work assignments are consistently below your capabilities, the result is 'rustout', which consists of boredom, fatigue, frustration and dissatisfaction. At the other extreme, when work assignments are consistently above your capabilities, the result is 'burnout', which was introduced in the previous chapter. Symptoms of burnout can often involve irrational problem-solving, exhaustion, illness and low self-esteem. Optimal performance at work is achieved by finding the correct level of stress, with enough stress to stimulate and motivate you, but not so much as to lead to burnout. This occurs when the work assignments are equal to your capabilities, leading to creativity, rational problem-solving, progress, change and satisfaction. This view is supported by research showing that teachers who take on additional duties in school guidance actually report lower levels of burnout than teachers who do not, despite the high rates of burnout prevalence among the population of teachers who took part in the research (Chan & Hui, 1995). However, stress from work overload among teachers is significantly higher than it is in other industries and, at the time of writing, work overload seems to be more of a stressor to teachers than work underload (National Union of Teachers, 1999; PricewaterhouseCoopers, 2001).

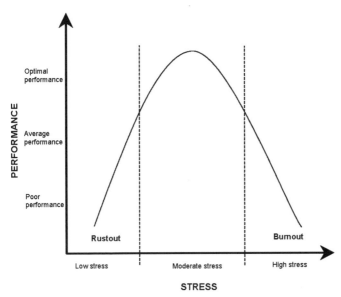

Illustration of the relationship between stress and performance

Positive and negative stress

Stress simply refers to your response to demands made on you, and is a necessary part of your life. However, the type and quality of stress you experience can be positive or negative.

Positive stress, also known as 'eustress', is the kind of stress you experience when you adapt positively to a challenge. Any satisfaction you get from putting effort into a task involves some positive stress.

Negative stress, also known as 'distress', is the kind of stress you experience when you feel under threat, out of control or stretched beyond your limits. Unpleasant feelings such as fear, anger and frustration tend to result from negative stress.

Eustress was a term first used by Selye (1956) to describe the way a certain amount of stress makes us perform better. The majority of literature on stress has focused on distress, and its negative effects. However, the research that has been conducted on eustress indicates that it has beneficial effects on the body as well as the mind. Consistent with the relationship between stress and performance, neurological research shows that mild to moderate stress actually improves memory, although severe and prolonged stress can seriously impair it (Sapolsky, 2004). Berk et al. (2001) found that humour resulted in several positive and significant effects on the immune system, which took effect immediately during laughter and lasted for at least 12 hours afterwards. Physiologically, during pleasure the body experiences moderate, unpredictable stress and pleasure is at its greatest when anticipating a reward, rather than while actually experiencing the reward (Sapolsky, 2004). In relation to work stress, Simmons & Nelson (2001) found that eustress in nurses was significantly related to positive perceptions of their own health. Their research indicates that engagement with even demanding work can lead to positive outcomes, even in highly stressful work environments. Furthermore, psychologists have recently developed theories of personal growth through adversity (Joseph & Linley, 2005), and a recent review indicated that the most effective stress-management approaches are those based on enhancing eustress (Le Fevre et al., 2006). Cavanaugh et al.

(2000) found that positive stress, termed 'challenge stress', was related to greater job satisfaction than negative stress, termed 'hindrance stress'. Therefore, there are many ways we can use stress to our advantage.

Stress, motivation and change

One of the really useful things about encountering a stressful situation is that your evaluation and interpretation of the stressful event can help bring about positive changes in your life. As you have seen from the research reported previously, your responses to stress can be positive or negative.

As you take in information from your own experiences and observations, from other people and from the environment, you are constantly making mental and emotional interpretations of it. These interpretations become integrated with your past experiences, and become part of your personal world view. However, your interpretations are not beyond your control. Therefore, in any stressful situation, it is important that you recognize your freedom to interpret the situation in a way that empowers you.

Interpreting situations positively involves recognizing how you want things to be different, thinking about how you could do things differently to bring this about and responding actively. Clarify the steps needed to make changes happen, and brainstorm and plan how you will carry out these steps. It is your choice whether you make changes in your life. It all depends on how you interpret the situation, whether your goals are achievable and how you feel about making those changes.

All too often, people under stress become acutely aware of the changes they would like to happen in their lives, but respond by ruminating and talking about the problems they are experiencing. As they grumble and complain about aspects of the stressful situation that are beyond their control, they negate any power they may actually have in the situation, and end up feeling tense, helpless, hopeless and ultimately burnt out. By responding passively, they accept the situation as it is, and therefore it does not change.

When you are under stress your body produces hormones such as adrenalin, which release physical energy, making you more alert and ready for action. When you interpret stress negatively, give up on any sense of control, respond passively and feel like a victim, the energy is not released, but your body is still prepared for action. You can end up literally losing sleep, worrying, fidgeting and holding tension in your body. In contrast, when you interpret stress positively, as a challenge, stressful situations can be a great source of energy to take action.

Once you have decided you do want to make a change, any further stress that results from a negative evaluation of what you are experiencing can become a useful reminder of what you are trying to achieve, and can promote further planning and task completion in working towards the changes you want to make. This is a way of maximizing the close relationship between stress and pleasure. According to Sapolsky (2004), to experience healthy stimulation it is important that the stress you are under is moderate, not high, and that the positive outcome you are working towards is achievable. On a physiological level, pleasure is at its greatest when success is strongly anticipated and likely to occur, but not entirely predictable.

How to know when you are under too much stress

The following questionnaire, or 'stress test', consists of a list of 20 statements for which you should choose 'yes' or 'no', depending on whether the statement is true for you. The scoring guidelines are on page 22. Please note that the stress test is not a scientifically validated test, it is simply an indicator that will help readers make sense of the material presented in this book. The stress test will help you to understand whether you are performing optimally, or whether you are under too much stress. Readers concerned about their stress levels are encouraged to seek professional help through their GP and/or a qualified psychologist, particularly if concerned about their score on the test.

The results of your stress test provide a 'snapshot' of how stressed you are at work, at the time of taking the test. As stressors in teaching vary according to factors such as the time of the academic year, you may find it helpful to take the test several times to get an indication of the range of stress you experience in your job as a whole.

Stress Test

1. I enjoy a laugh and a joke with my students and/or colleagues most days.	Yes/No
2. I don't have the time or the inclination to try and enjoy myself at work.	Yes/No
3. I believe my students will succeed in their qualifications and go on to do well.	Yes/No
4. I think many of my students do not have the ability or motivation to complete their qualifications to a high standard.	Yes/No
5. I usually feel in control in my interactions with students.	Yes/No
6. Many students do not respect the staff or the rules of the school.	Yes/No
7. At least one of my colleagues makes my life difficult by undermining me.	Yes/No
8. I have experienced some form of bullying or harassment from students or colleagues, such as making racially or sexually inappropriate comments, undermining my competence, or criticizing my personality.	Yes/No
9. I have more work to do than I can comfortably cope with.	Yes/No
10. My job has become tedious and repetitive.	Yes/No
11. There are not enough hours in the day to do everything, so I sometimes have to take work home with me and work on it during evenings, weekends and holidays.	Yes/No
12. I usually feel on top of my work.	Yes/No
13. It bothers me, or would bother me, if my boss checked up on me often.	Yes/No
14. I feel I can manage my own stress by taking care over my work.	Yes/No

15. I drink caffeine to help me cope with the demands of   Yes/No
    my job and/or I find alcoholic drinks help me
    unwind after a stressful day at work.
16. I take sleeping pills and/or anti-depressants and/or   Yes/No
    other medication to help me cope.
17. I take painkillers quite often to deal with headaches   Yes/No
    or backache.
18. I take an enjoyable form of exercise at least once a week. Yes/No
19. I am often too tired to eat properly, and may skip meals, Yes/No
    eat a lot of snacks or eat junk food.
20. I feel I spend enough enjoyable time with my family,   Yes/No
    friends or social group.

Scoring

Add up your score using the following key. Watch out for minus points for some items. When you have worked out your score, look up which scoring range you currently fall into.

1. Yes = −1, No = 1	11. Yes = 1, No = 0
2. Yes = 1, No = 0	12. Yes = 0, No = 1
3. Yes = −1, No = 1	13. Yes = 1, No = 0
4. Yes = 1, No = 0	14. Yes = 0, No = 1
5. Yes = −1, No = 1	15. Yes = 1, No = 0
6. Yes = 1, No = 0	16. Yes = 1, No = 0
7. Yes = 1, No = 0	17. Yes = 1, No = 0
8. Yes = 1, No = 0	18. Yes = −1, No = 1
9. Yes = 1, No = 0	19. Yes = 1, No = 0
10. Yes = 1, No = 0	20. Yes = 0, No = 1

Scoring ranges

4–0: Low distress, high eustress

Not only are you doing all the right things to manage your stress, you are also experiencing aspects of positive stress such as hope and humour. You may be contented, or you may want to consider seeking more stimulation or challenge in your work.

0–5: Low stress

Generally you find your job causes you relatively little stress and you may find that aspects of positive stress, such as hope and humour, make your work more enjoyable. Think about whether you are contented, would like more challenge or are feeling fulfilled in other areas of your life.

5–10: Moderate stress

Your work life has a balance between times of stimulation and times of stress. If you are comfortable with the kinds of challenges you are experiencing, you may be functioning optimally.

10–15: High stress

Your work life is becoming stressful to the extent that it is likely to be impacting on other areas of your life, and your functioning may not be at the level you are capable of. Try some of the stress-management techniques described in this book. If you are already following the advice in this book, it may be that your job is creating more stress than you can comfortably cope with and it may be time to consider a change in role.

15–20: Extreme stress

Your stress level is extremely high. If this is an ongoing situation, you should seek help and support in managing your stress as soon as possible. Begin to incorporate the techniques described in this book into your routine. You may also benefit from the support of a counsellor and should discuss your current life situation with your doctor, who may be able to help or may be able to refer you to someone who can. If you do not take action soon, you may find the levels of stress you are experiencing will take a toll on your long-term health.

What to do if you are under too much stress

Remember, the harmful effects of stress are caused not only by how much stress you are under, but also by how you interpret and appraise that stress. A moderate amount of stress, particularly 'positive' stress, is healthy and stimulating.

There are two aspects of dealing effectively with stress: dealing with the causes and dealing with the symptoms. It is important not to overwhelm yourself by trying to change too much at once – if this is a tendency of yours, it may have contributed to your stress in the first place! So start with some basic approaches to dealing with the symptoms of stress, and then move on to thinking about and addressing the causes. Dealing with the symptoms of stress first will make you feel healthier, more energetic and more empowered. You will then have the mental, emotional and physical resources to tackle the causes of your stress.

However, the two aspects of dealing with stress are not mutually exclusive. Consider, for example, a symptom of stress such as backache. Pain in your back for an extended period of time can become a stressor in itself, particularly if it starts interfering with other activities that help alleviate stress, such as exercise. Similarly, a cause of stress, such as a hostile work environment, may be a reflection of the symptoms of stress being experienced by people within that environment. So it is mainly for the sake of clarity that strategies for dealing with the symptoms of stress will be presented first, followed by strategies for dealing with the causes of stress.

Managing the symptoms of stress in teaching

Action plan:

- Step 1: Develop a positive attitude.
- Step 2: Practise stress-management skills.
- Step 3: Identify sources of support.
- Step 4: Learn effective communication skills.

Step 1: Develop a positive attitude

As described earlier, stressors can be interpreted either positively or negatively, and positive forms of stress are actually important for getting the most out of your career. There is mounting evidence that positive stress (eustress) is good for your health (Berk et al., 2001), whereas negative stress (distress) has the opposite effect (Sapolsky, 2004). While some situations are undeniably unpleasant, there are many that simply require self-belief, hope or humour to change your interpretation from negative to positive.

Rydstedt et al. (2004) found that what people believe about the causes and alleviation of work-related stress was significantly related to the actual stress and mental strain they were experiencing over a year later. When people believed job stress was caused by danger or pressure at work, they reported more job stress. Those that believed demographic differences, such as age and gender, caused job stress reported more mental strain over a year later. In contrast, the researchers also found that there were certain beliefs that were associated with lower stress. People who believed that taking care over their work prevents job stress and those who thought it was important to be checked up on by superiors actually reported less job stress and mental strain at follow-up.

It is interesting to consider the differences between these two sets of beliefs. When you believe that stress at work is caused by factors that are beyond your control, such as danger, age or gender, you actually experience more stress and mental strain for a prolonged period of time. On the other hand, when you believe that stress is not only caused by factors within your control, but can also be prevented by specific behaviours you can take responsibility for, such as taking care or being checked up on by superiors, you experience less stress and mental strain. It is particularly interesting to note that when you recognize the role your superiors have in preventing stress by checking up on you, you access the stress-reducing effects of the positive interpretation of a situation that could be interpreted negatively, as well as probably developing a better relationship with your boss. This is likely to reduce your stress even more, by creating a collaborative and trusting working relationship. This has tremendous implications for understanding the different attitudes teachers have towards the school inspection process, as well as their experiences and responses to inspection.

There is mounting evidence that a positive attitude can alleviate stress. Blix et al. (1994) found that university teachers who believe they can manage work stress have fewer stress symptoms. Therefore a first step towards managing the symptoms of stress is to develop positive beliefs about your ability to effectively manage stress at work. Examples of how this might be accomplished include developing a belief in our ability to ensure our own well-being, and positively interpreting a manager's interest in work performance, rather than viewing such interest as a threat or intrusion.

The following points show ways in which you can develop a positive attitude towards stress:

- *Consciously enjoy your 'eustress',* such as the positive feelings of stimulation and accomplishment that come with putting effort into your job. For example, rather than giving in to feelings of anxiety when going into a new class, allow yourself to feel the excitement of discovering a group of unique individuals with the potential to learn all you have to teach them.

- *Assess your beliefs about stress.* Re-interpret those that feel out of your control as presenting you with more opportunities. For example, if you feel a particular class is always a challenge recognize the professional skills and abilities such a challenge is developing in you, and how that is broadening your understanding as a teacher. Remember that this breadth of experience will serve you well when you are promoted.

- *Consciously acknowledge the advantages* of your age, your gender, your culture and ethnic group, your social background, your abilities and your disabilities. Each of these characteristics will provide you with special insights that contribute to your school, and provide good role modelling for your students. For example, you may feel disadvantaged by having a learning disability. However, this gives you a much greater level of empathy with your students as they struggle to learn, and particularly those who have learning disabilities. This empathy can make you a more understanding teacher than others who have never had this experience, leading to a better rapport and stronger relationships with your students. It also makes you a positive role model to students with learning disabilities.

- *Recognize that you can accomplish everything* your job demands and everything you require of yourself. You may need more time and support to do so, but if it is important you accomplish the task, that time and support will need to be made available to you. The time and support staff needs of teachers are now being recognized, and reflected in the *National Agreement* (described in more detail on pages 31–2). There are also tips throughout this book on how you can make these more available to yourself.
- *Maintain a sense of hope and a sense of humour.* Both are important aspects of positive stress (Simmons & Nelson, 2001; Berk et al., 2001) and make your life a lot more fun!

Step 2: Practice stress-management skills

Research studies evaluating the effectiveness of stress-management strategies show that the development of skills such as relaxation (Reynolds et al., 1993; Teasdale et al., 2000; Heron et al. 1999), time management (Reynolds et al., 1993) and even exercise (Whatmore et al., 1999) assisted individuals with workplace stress. These skills can be self-taught, and the following pages will get you started with some simple and practical guidelines on relaxation, time management and exercise, which can easily be integrated into your current lifestyle.

Two-minute relaxation exercise

This exercise is very simple and can be practised anywhere and at any time. It can be adapted to the situation you are in by shortening or extending it, depending on what is appropriate in the circumstances. It is quite possible to do this exercise during your working day, in those brief moments during teaching when students are involved in small-group activity, or while they are focused on reading material. Equally, this exercise can be conducted for an hour or more while lying down at home. It is an excellent insomnia cure!

1. *Get comfortable*

    If possible, sit down with your feet flat on the floor and your legs comfortably apart. If standing, balance the weight of your body between both feet and 'unlock' your knees by bending them slightly, while keeping them springy. Allow your hands, arms and shoulders to relax. If lying down, try to lie on your back with your weight distributed evenly, with your arms and legs relaxed and open. These slight changes to your posture will begin to make you feel more relaxed straight away.

2. *Notice your breathing*

    When you are stressed your body automatically changes your breathing pattern, speeding it up and emphasizing inhalation. This is the body's natural way of attempting to increase the oxygen supply to the bloodstream. However, in a school environment, with no opportunity to work off the stress physically, this often leads to poor breathing habits that prevent relaxation. Notice if you are holding your breath at all, if your breathing is shallow or rapid or if you feel you just can't take a proper deep breath. Relax your diaphragm by letting go of any tightness just where your ribs meet. Allow your stomach to relax and to move gently as you breathe in and out.

3. *Body scan*

    Mentally scan your body from the head down or the feet up. As you notice any areas of tension, consciously relax those areas by letting the muscle go loose. Common areas to hold tension without realizing it are: the forehead, the jaw, the shoulders, stomach, the pelvic area, the knees and the feet. With practice, you will get to know the areas where you hold tension, and it will become easier to let them relax during the body scan.

4. *Lengthen your exhalation*

    This is where the magic happens! Your pattern of breathing is directly linked to your nervous system's control of the stress response, so you can change how relaxed you feel simply by changing the pattern of your breathing. One of the quickest and easiest ways to accomplish this is simply to breathe out more slowly, and for a longer period of time. People vary in terms of how easy they find it to control their breathing but try to extend your exhalation (breathing out) for at least a count of five, longer if you can manage it. With practice, you can extend each exhalation for a count of ten. Don't worry about extending your inhalation, simply relax and allow your lungs to fill up naturally. As long as your body remains relaxed and comfortable, very quickly you will feel calmer and your body will relax further. Keep up the extended exhalation breathing pattern for two minutes, or as long as you wish to relax.

Other relaxation skills to try

The skills that follow, and many others, are described in more detail in *The relaxation and stress reduction workbook* by Davis et al. (2000).

Progressive Muscle Relaxation (PMR)

This involves working through the different muscle groups of the body in sequence, becoming aware of and then relaxing them. For the full effect it is best practised in a focused way for 15 minutes or more but, once you learn the technique, simplified versions can be practised at work for shorter periods of time. PMR is also effective practised in a group setting or listening to an instruction tape. A digital recording of the author providing PMR instructions can be downloaded from www.drhartney.com.

Meditation

This is based on ancient religious practices, but there are many types of meditation that can be practised alone or in groups. Meditation consists of relaxing physically, while becoming very focused mentally. Meditation is a very useful way of tackling the tendency always to be busy or in control, as the goal is to develop a sense of letting things be as they are. Regular meditation practice can completely change your attitude to yourself and the world around you. However, it can be challenging to learn for some people. Simple instructions for understanding the basics and beginning meditation can be found at www.meditationcenter.com.

Self-hypnosis

Hypnosis involves using the power of suggestion to change behaviour. Although hypnotism can be carried out by a hypnotist or hypnotherapist, it is quite possible to learn to hypnotize yourself. People vary in their ability to be hypnotized but hypnosis is extremely effective in the management of stress, along with many other behaviours that involve self-control, such as smoking, weight loss and skills development. An excellent book that explains simple, safe approaches is *Stress Control Through Self-Hypnosis* by Jackson (1993).

What is time management?

Time-management behaviours have been shown to reduce job-related tension and physical tension, increase job satisfaction and to enhance feelings of control over time (Macan, 1994). Jex and Elacqua (1999) found that using time-management behaviours can have a strong effect on whether stressors such as role conflict, role overload and conflicts between family and work actually result in stress in employed people.

It is important to be as realistic about what you cannot do as what you can do, in a given period of time. A study of teachers' workload found that teachers' working weeks are more intensive than most other occupations, with 50 to 60 hours being the norm at the time of writing (PricewaterhouseCoopers, 2001). This study found that teachers were burdened with many unnecessary tasks that distracted them from teaching, for up to two-thirds of their working time and that they often lacked the skills to manage staff and other resources at their disposal. As a result of this study, and after sustained pressure from teachers' leaders for action to address excessive teacher workload, the government accepted there was a need to introduce workload-cutting measures. *Raising standards and tackling workload: a national agreement* was signed by the government, employers and teacher unions in January 2003 (ATL et al., 2003).

The *National Agreement* identified 25 administrative tasks that teachers now have a contractual right not to carry out, even if requested to do so by management (Teacher Support Network, 2006). These tasks are:

1. collecting money;
2. chasing absences – teachers will need to inform the relevant member of staff when students are absent from their class or from school;
3. bulk photocopying;
4. copy typing;
5. producing standard letters – teachers may be required to contribute as appropriate in formulating the content of standard letters;
6. producing class lists – teachers may be required to be involved as appropriate in allocating students to a particular class;
7. record keeping and filing – teachers may be required to contribute to the content of records;
8. classroom display – teachers will make professional decisions in determining what material is displayed in and around their classroom;
9. analysing attendance figures – it is for teachers to make use of the outcome of analysis;
10. processing exam results – teachers will need to use the analysis of exam results;
11. collating pupil reports;
12. administering work experience – teachers may be required to support pupils on work experience (including through advice and visits);
13. administering examinations – teachers have a professional responsibility for identifying appropriate examinations for their pupils;
14. invigilating examinations (see district provisions);
15. administering teacher cover;

16. ICT troubleshooting and minor repairs;
17. commissioning new ICT equipment;
18. ordering supplies and equipment – teachers may be involved in identifying needs;
19. stocktaking;
20. cataloguing, preparing, issuing and maintaining equipment and materials;
21. minuting meetings – teachers may be required to communicate action points from meetings;
22. coordinating and submitting bids – teachers may be required to make a professional input into the content of bids;
23. seeking and giving personnel advice;
24. managing pupil data – teachers will need to make use of the analysis of pupil data;
25. inputting pupil data – teachers will need to make the initial entry of pupil data into school management systems.

Although you may need to work on relationships at work (see Chapter 5) and improve your ability to deal with difficult people (see Chapter 6), you are strongly encouraged to begin making maximum use of support staff such as teaching and administrative assistants (National Union of Teachers, 1999). This will free up more time to focus on teaching and marking. Development of good time-management skills can help alleviate the stress of having too much to do in too little time.

The *National Agreement* also stated that teachers should rarely be asked to cover for absent colleagues, and the number of hours of cover they provide should not exceed 38 per year. Also, all teachers, including headteachers, should have a reasonable work/life balance (see Chapter 7). Furthermore, all teachers will have guaranteed (timetabled) planning, preparation and assessment (PPA) time of at least 10 per cent of their work time (half a day a week for a full-time teacher).

Time-management skills include behaviours such as:

- *Goal setting* – this involves deciding what to accomplish from the beginning. For example, your goal might be to write your lesson plans for the week ahead. Each intended lesson plan is one goal. The trick to making goals work is to stick to them! If you shut out distractions and focus on one goal at a time, you will be amazed at how much can be achieved.

- *Prioritization* – next, decide which goals are most important and should be dealt with first. For example, you might have three lesson plans to prepare for the week ahead, but the first lesson is the most important one to prepare right now, as it will be needed first. If you are interrupted, or run out of time, you at least have your first lesson prepared, and can still make time to prepare the next one later.

- *'Mechanics' of time management* – these are the behaviours that facilitate the process of time management. Continuing with the example of lesson plans, it is helpful to use a template with mini-prompts for yourself for completing the plan. Then make copies of the blank template and fill them in for each lesson. You may have to invest a little more time initially getting the template prepared, but you will save a great deal of time once you start using it. An added bonus is that your lesson plans will be neat and consistent. You can also save enormous amounts of time by using lesson plans that have already been created according to National Curriculum criteria, and approved by teachers, by searching the database of over 2,000 lesson plans at:
  http://www.teachernet.gov.uk/teachingandlearning/resourcematerials/Resources/

- *Organization* – this involves taking an organized, methodical approach to work. For lesson-plan preparation, keeping your syllabus, course dates and course outline together in one place, such as a ring binder, along with your old lesson plans and a supply of blank templates, and always keeping it in the same place so that you never lose it, will greatly speed up the process. It might also be helpful to set a specific time each week to work on your lesson plans, such as during your timetabled PPA time. It will also help if you can set yourself a certain amount of time to spend on each lesson plan and stick to it. This should not exceed the time recommended by the school (and what you are paid for). A simple way of estimating how long to spend on preparation, marking and so on is to divide the number of tasks by the amount of time you have scheduled. If it is taking longer, you should consider whether your personal standards are higher than what is actually required. Excessive planning in particular may be more related to your own perfectionism than necessity, as most teachers have sufficient knowledge of their subject and the curriculum to teach the occasional lesson with minimal planning.

Exercise

Exercise helps with the management of stress in several ways. On a physical level, it releases endorphins, the body's natural painkillers, which promote pleasant physical and emotional feelings. Exercise brings the nervous system into balance, inducing the relaxation response, which is important for sleep, digestion and emptying the mind of worries and anxieties. It also tightens and releases the muscles, relieving tension and allowing them to relax fully afterwards. On a mental level, exercise focuses your attention on something other than your stressors, giving you a break from thinking about worries and concerns. On an emotional level, many forms of exercise are fun, and there is a form of exercise that is enjoyable for all personality types. Exercise also supports you emotionally through the sense of empowerment that comes with taking control of your health and happiness, rather than feeling like a victim of circumstance.

Exercise to incorporate into your working day could include the following:

- *Treadmill*: Walk or cycle to work, or part of the way to work, instead of driving or taking public transport.
- *Step aerobics*: Take the stairs instead of the lift. Walk with a straight back, and allow your legs to be springy.
- *Weights*: Invest in two identical bags with comfortable handles. Distribute your marking, books and so on equally between the two bags. Carry with your arms hanging loosely by your sides, your back straight and your legs relaxed and springy.

Exercise to consider out of work

There are many types of exercise to consider out of work. The following suggestions are excellent for stress management, and are presented from the least to the most strenuous. While the more gentle forms of exercise are calming, the more strenuous activities can be particularly effective in providing an outlet for pent-up frustration, as long as you *let go* of the feelings as you exercise, rather than intensifying and building them up. You should always consult your doctor before starting a new exercise programme.

- yoga
- t'ai chi
- walking
- swimming
- dancing
- skating
- aerobics
- weights
- running
- team sports
- boxing/kick-boxing.

Joining a gym or an exercise class can be a good way of incorporating exercise into your leisure time, but it is not the only way to get regular exercise. There are many videos and DVDs on the market, offering expert tuition on different types of exercise. Some of the workouts available, such as the *10-minute solution* series (see Further resources, page 154), are as short as 10 minutes so they can easily be incorporated into your daily routine. Ten minutes of exercise practised before your morning shower on weekdays adds up to 50 minutes a week, which is roughly equivalent to a weekly exercise class. Even with just 10 minutes of exercise a day, you will notice immediate improvement in your mood, energy and sense of accomplishment.

An even shorter option is the *4 Minute Fitness*™ approach, which incorporates t'ai chi, yoga, meditation and ancient qi gong (chi kung), combined with modern medical theories, relaxation methods and motivational techniques (see page 154). The approach has been shown by research to reduce teacher stress (Jefferey, 2002) and teachers report successfully practising it with their students at the beginning of lessons.

Step 3: Identify sources of support

The next step in addressing the symptoms of stress is to find out about sources of support. Many studies show that supportive services provided by employers, such as cognitive-behaviour therapy and counselling, significantly improve workers' ability to manage work-related stress (Bond & Bunce, 2000; Cooper & Sadri, 1991; Firth-Cozens & Hardy, 1992; Michie, 1992, 1996) and psychotherapy is effective in alleviating the symptoms of burnout (Salmela-Aro et al., 2004). Rational Emotive Therapy has been identified as particularly effective in assisting teachers in dealing with stress (Forman, 1990). This approach uses a stress-inoculation training framework and provides behavioural and cognitive-behavioural coping skills, which can be used to alter psychological and physiological responses to potential stressors and negative stress reactions.

The Teacher Support Line can provide immediate counselling support on the telephone, 24 hours a day. They can refer you to face-to-face counselling if appropriate. You might also find coaching helpful, which is also provided by the Teacher Support Line. Alternatively, you might find it more helpful to contact your union for support. Other sources of counselling and psychotherapy can be accessed through Saneline, who have a national database containing details of many different services, and who can advise you on those specific to your needs and locale. Contact details of all of these sources of support are included in Further Resources (pages 149–55), and more details of different ways of finding help are included in Chapter 8.

Step 4: Learn effective communication skills

The next step in managing stress at work is to develop and practise good communication skills. One of the best places to start is by developing your 'emotional intelligence'. Emotional intelligence refers to intelligence that is specific to social interactions and, in particular, the ability to recognize and respond appropriately to your own and other people's emotions (Goleman, 1996). Communication skills that facilitate emotional intelligence include listening skills, expressive skills and empathy. The importance of developing emotional intelligence in combating workplace bullying is detailed in Sheehan (1999).

Kremenitzer (2005) identified four domains of emotional intelligence skills important for teachers to develop: perception skills, accessing skills, understanding skills and regulation skills. Perception skills involve identifying what you and other people are feeling, and in particular noticing when your students are angry, sad, bored and so on. Accessing skills involve the ability to access different feelings as they relate to thinking, for example to talk yourself through a negative mood or to know the best time for students to be motivated to complete certain projects. Understanding skills involve using the right words and helping students find the right words to describe feelings accurately, and recognizing and making sense of different emotional reactions in yourself and your students. Regulation skills involve being able to cope with the unexpected, and to be able to self-regulate and role-model self-regulation to students in difficult circumstances.

One of the most important communication skills is listening. Listening might seem an obvious and straightforward part of your daily interactions, but many people never actually develop good listening skills. In fact, according to Held (1996) there is a good chance that while you think you are listening to someone, you are actually wearing a 'listening mask'. You wear a listening mask to look as if you are listening when you are doing something else mentally, such as daydreaming, faking attention (either deliberately or on 'autopilot'), being distracted by something other than the speaker, protecting yourself from the speaker, selectively listening only to the information you want to (and ignoring the rest) and mind-reading (assuming you know what the other person is saying rather than listening to what they actually are saying).

Ensuring that you have understood the other person's message, and making sure the other person has understood your message, is central to good communication. Here are some tips for good communication:

- Encourage the other person to talk first (but you go first if the other person seems reluctant).
- Focus on the content of what the person is saying, and different things it could mean, rather than simply waiting for your own turn to talk.
- Before stating your own point of view, paraphrase what the other person said and ask if that was, in fact, what they meant.
- Pay attention to the other person's feelings, as well as the content of what they are saying. Show some understanding, verbally or non-verbally.
- When it is your turn to speak, keep things simple. Don't waffle around with unnecessary apologies, background information or anything else that might confuse the other person and prevent them from focusing on your message.
- At the end of the conversation, reiterate any agreements made (or the lack of agreement and why), and any further action to be taken.
- Be specific about future action, for example if you agree to discuss the matter again, set a specific time/date/place, and be clear about whether it is a firm arrangement or a tentative one.

There are always times when good communication is not enough to avoid disagreements, and many people are anxious about running into conflict with others. Edelmann (1993) suggested the use of negotiating and bargaining as a strategy for dealing with conflict. This enables both parties to reach a joint decision on how they can work together. This can be achieved through four steps.

Steps for conflict resolution

- recognizing the problem
- understanding each other's position
- discussing the problem and possible solutions
- resolving the problem in a mutually acceptable way.

The use of negotiation and bargaining when conflicts are experienced with colleagues, students and others is helpful, particularly in situations where change is preferable to avoidance (see next section and Chapter 5). Although the steps appear straightforward, people often become emotional and self-righteous during the process, so it can be helpful to have someone mediate the process. The role of the mediator is not to take turns but to enable each person to express their point of view, and to ensure that the discussion stays focused on finding a solution without escalating into an argument. You can find out more about the mediation process through the Advisory, Conciliation and Arbitration Service (ACAS), who can also offer advice and mediation services. Their details are in Further resources (pages 151–2) and at www.acas.org.uk.

Managing the causes of stress in teaching

Action plan:

- Step 1: Identify whether you have 'burnout' or 'rustout'.
- Step 2: Evaluate your workplace culture.
- Step 3: Consider discussing stress with your manager.
- Step 4: Time to stop or time to go?

Step 1: Identify whether you have 'burnout' or 'rustout'

As discussed in Chapter 1, it is important to identify what kind of stress you are experiencing. Gmelch (1983) argued that approaches to managing the stress of 'burnout' and the stress of 'rustout' are different.

In cases of burnout, you can take positive steps to decrease daily exposure to high levels of stress. Gmelch (1983) gives examples of how this might be accomplished, including: breaking up continuous people contacts; knowing and understanding the stress your job entails; saying no; delegating responsibility; and breaking up larger projects into smaller parts. In the school environment, this may seem difficult to accomplish. However, small changes in your working routine can make a big difference to the stress you experience. A ten-minute break for example, which could be accomplished by taking a short walk or finding a quiet space to relax, can allow your body's fight or flight response to diminish, and your breathing, heart rate, sweat glands and so on to return to normal. You will then find it easier to stay more relaxed later on.

Research by PricewaterhouseCoopers (2001) indicates that burnout in teachers is much more likely than rustout. However, there are individuals who experience rustout for various reasons, such as being new to the job, changes in staffing and lack of direction from management. In these cases, you are encouraged to practise assertiveness, and to ask for the direction and information you need to make progress (see Chapter 6). Rustout may also occur in teachers who have become familiar with teaching responsibilities but lack the initiative to engage in new areas of work. In cases of rustout, Gmelch (1983) suggests actually increasing stress intake. This could include: staying alert; taking risks; avoiding isolation; stretching for success; and overcoming obsolescence. Kyriacou (2001) suggests taking on duties in a valued area of work may enhance job satisfaction, even in the context of a heavy workload.

Even if you do not want to take on any extra teaching, you could look into contributing to new directions in the school, perhaps in an advisory capacity. This will provide stimulation and help you and others to appreciate the value of your experience. Another option would be to look into taking a further or higher education course yourself, perhaps in IT or the growing field of e-learning. Many are available online and your new skills would be an asset to your employer. Both of these strategies increase professional recognition and contribute to your chances of future promotion, and are encouraged in the *National Agreement*.

To maintain peak performance, Gmelch (1983) suggests: establishing goals; taking control of time; maintaining sound health; and knowing your own stress points. You will find many practical strategies for following Gmelch's advice throughout this book.

Step 2: Evaluate your workplace culture

The source of your stress may not be the work itself, but the workplace culture. Culture includes shared language, beliefs and practices among a group of people with something in common. There are many reasons for a culture of stress developing in the workplace, which commonly happens when employees are implicitly or explicitly rewarded for maintaining the appearance of high levels of stress in the workplace, and punished for appearing calm at work.

Sometimes a culture of stress can develop around teachers' attitudes towards aspects of their work, particularly inspection. Ball (2003) presented two contrasting cultural extremes. One is the culture of 'performativity', in which teachers focus on competitiveness, accountability, performance, targets and incentives, in which 'value replaces values' and there is 'no room for caring'. The other is the culture of teachers under stress, who are forced into compromising their values, creativity, professional integrity and 'the children', leaving them racked with shame, guilt and a lack of self-respect. They resent 'playing the game', which is described as 'licking their [Ofsted's] boots', and ultimately take a stand by leaving the profession.

These kinds of stereotypical portrayals of teachers are quite unhelpful in stress management, as they encourage teachers to identify with one or the other (and readers are implicitly encouraged to identify with the stressed, caring teachers). In reality, all teachers balance the need for accountability and improvement of their practice with values of caring and relationship building to a greater or lesser extent. In contrast with Ball's (2003) portrayal of the 'performative' culture as being uncaring about teachers and children, recent advances in the development of teacher's roles, reflected in the *National Agreement*, the *Every Child Matters* initiative and many other initiatives discussed elsewhere in this book, show that society is committed to supporting teachers and enhancing opportunities and care for children.

Yet these stereotypical portrayals of teachers are quite pervasive in teaching culture and, in addition to the 'rewards and sanctions' Ball (2003) describes for teachers' adherence to the 'culture of performativity', rewards and punishments within the culture of individual schools can take many different forms, which may create and maintain collective stress. Some common ones are listed below:

How stress can be encouraged in the school culture

- *People who resist change and criticize the system are seen as having integrity.* This is like Ball's (2003) portrayal of the stressed teacher.
- *People who embrace change and work within national established frameworks are seen as lacking integrity.* The many benefits of systems of school improvement are missed, as teachers cling to such ideas as anything originating with the government must be immoral and regarded with suspicion, teachers must fabricate their professional activities to survive and focusing on children's achievement is harmful to their relationships with teachers.
- *People who appear stressed are perceived as working hard.* The reward of appearing stressed may be an improved reputation for hard work, the ability to take the credit for shared tasks and a means of covering up incompetence and laziness.
- *People who appear calm are perceived as lazy.* They may be punished by their work not being recognized as their own, their job being considered to be easy and they may be overlooked for promotion or perks.
- *People who appear stressed can avoid taking on extra tasks.* Managers and peers may fear they will be pushed 'over the edge' if they take on any more, thus those who appear stressed may avoid their fair share of the workload.

- *People who appear calm are perceived as not having enough to do.* In some workplaces you are not considered to be pulling your weight unless you have *more* work than you can cope with.
- *Stress can become a way for staff to communicate their dissatisfaction* to others. This is particularly the case when the workplace culture has taboos against the discussion of certain topics, which may in fact be the source of people's unhappiness.
- *The language of stress can become a way that staff communicate their anxieties* to one another. It can provide one another with a sense of support, without having to talk about their actual feelings or concerns.
- *Staff may be praised for hard work, working under pressure or meeting unreasonable targets rather than the quality or even the quantity of their work.* This is particularly harmful in under-staffed environments.

There are also cultures and subcultures among teachers, such as subject subcultures (Goodson & Mangan, 1995), and teachers are sometimes able to justify their resistance to even clearly defined roles and responsibilities by reinterpretation and professional justification grounded in the culture of teaching (Shimahara & Sakai, 1992). Some school cultures are still overtly racist, as Miller and Travers' (2005) research showed that ethnic minority teachers in the UK were more stressed and less satisfied than other teachers, some reporting daily discrimination and institutional racism. In these circumstances government initiatives, as well as teachers' unions, provide excellent opportunities for redress. Advisory, Conciliation and Arbitration Service (ACAS) may also be able to help if you are suffering from discrimination at work (see Further resources, pages 151–2, for more details).

In understanding and addressing the sources of your stress at work, it is helpful to assess whether any of the above, or any other aspect of your workplace culture, is maintaining your stress at work. If so, it is important to separate yourself psychologically from this culture. You can choose to maintain the appearance of stress if it is important for self-protection in a pro-stress workplace culture, without actually being stressed. For example, you can use the shared language of stress in your department without actually having to go through the stress yourself. It may be that in reality many of your peers are doing exactly the same thing.

If you are in a position to influence the workplace culture, you may even be able to make it more acceptable to appear less stressed. This is particularly the case if you are in any kind of management, health and safety or employee representative role, in which case you can even be quite open about your goal to change the workplace culture around stress. However, for this to be effective, you will need to make it psychologically safe for other staff to cooperate. If they fear it is another ploy to give them more to do, they will retaliate and cause you much more stress.

Step 3: Consider discussing stress with your manager

Discussing stress with your manager should be approached with care and forethought. A key aspect in recent compensation claims that have been won by teachers who endured extreme stress was that they had approached their manager, explained they were under extreme stress and needed support and were not given adequate support to prevent them from becoming ill (Judd, 1999; Wade & Dyer, 2003). Therefore, if you believe you are suffering from work-related stress, which is at an unacceptable level, you should not only report this to your manager and ask for steps to be taken to address it, but you should also keep meticulous records of doing so, and the outcome. Raising issues of staff stress at meetings that are minuted is also a good way of ensuring that your requests and any responses are documented, which will support your case if at a later point you wish to take the matter further.

Your employer has a responsibility to ensure you work under safe and healthy conditions, and the Health and Safety Executive (HSE) has put together a package to help organizations to meet their duty of care and their duty to assess for risk of work-related stress (Health and Safety Executive, 2003). Therefore you do have a right to have your concerns about stress addressed. However, diplomacy should also be exercised when doing so. On one hand you need to protect yourself and ensure that you are not expected to tolerate unreasonable levels of stress, by communicating your needs to your manager (which they are obliged to address). On the other hand teaching is intrinsically stressful and even the National Teachers' Union, perhaps the teacher's greatest advocate for reducing stressful working conditions, proposes that teachers do all they can to manage their own stress (National Union of Teachers, 1999).

Even the best managers vary greatly in terms of how they perceive stress, and some hold negative views of stress, such as perceiving complaints of stress as an excuse for weakness or incompetence, or a threat to the smooth running of the school. In any event, managers are typically functioning at extreme levels of stress themselves (PricewaterhouseCooper, 2001), with complaints of stress from staff adding to their own stress. Without placing any judgements, it is often easier to resolve the issue yourself. That way you can avoid further stress related to the reactions of others. The *National Agreement* provides greater support to teachers in avoiding stress, but it also gives more responsibility to teachers to utilize it to manage their own stress. For example, the *National Agreement* supports you in refusing to do any of the 25 tasks listed earlier on in this chapter. However, you do have the responsibility to delegate those tasks to a support staff member. Some teachers, at least initially, will find delegation more difficult than carrying out routine administrative tasks themselves. If this is the case for you, recognize your own professional status and read Chapters 5 and 6, which will help you develop the skills needed in delegation.

If you feel you need to involve your manager in helping you address your problems with stress, it can help to present your experiences of stress along with solutions that you think might help resolve the problems. If you are doing any of the 25 tasks that teachers are not required to carry out, state clearly what you are doing and why you are doing it. A potential solution might involve having the manager's support or direct input in delegating the task to a more appropriate member of support staff (for example, if you have attempted to do so yourself unsuccessfully), or recruiting more support staff to help.

Another way to address the issue of stress management is to align your request with the school's goals. Ofsted (2005) reported that very few schools tackled mental health problems, and only a third of secondary schools visited taught Personal, Social and Health Education (PSHE) programmes that included stress. They also stated that just over half of the schools included in this report were aware of the National Healthy School Standards (NHSS). The National Healthy Schools Programme is focused on improving physical and emotional health in the whole school community – from parents to governors to school staff. Furthermore, Ofsted (2005) stated that positive behaviour requires an active, whole-school approach to developing children's social, emotional and behavioural skills within a community that promotes the emotional well-being of all its members. By introducing stress-management strategies for staff, the school can effectively demonstrate its commitment to a whole-school approach to wellness. Teachers will be role-modelling good stress-management skills, development to students, and this will provide evidence that the school is committed to the well-being of all its members, including teachers.

Some acceptable stress-management approaches you could suggest to your manager, which would fit these criteria, are to:

- *Become a 'Healthy School'* through the National Healthy Schools Programme. It addresses the whole-school community, including staff, and many of the standards reflect behavioural changes advocated in this book. This will raise the profile of the school and reflect well in the school's Ofsted report. More details are available at the Healthy Schools website at www.healthyschools.gov.uk.
- *Start a relaxation group* at lunchtime or after work. This could include working through some simple relaxation exercises such as those described in Chapter 2. You might approach your manager to ask for approval and use of school facilities such as the gym and audio-visual equipment.
- *Start an exercise group* at lunchtime or after work. This could include an exercise class with an instructor, or simply using a DVD. As with the relaxation group, you might approach your

manager and ask for use of school facilities. This would meet the specific National Healthy School Standard of all staff engaging in physical exercise.

- *Arrange a 4 minute fitness*® *workshop for staff, or use the DVD.* This approach combines relaxation skills, motivational skills and exercise. The fact that this approach has been shown to be effective in reducing stress in teachers (Jefferey, 2002), and teachers even report success in practising with students at the beginning of lessons, adds weight to this as an appropriate choice. The workshops are also reported to be effective in teambuilding. More details are available in Further resources (page 154), and through the website at www.4minutefitness.com.
- *Professional development opportunities.* You could suggest time management as a possible professional development course, either for yourself or for your colleagues.
- *Increasing your own 'eustress'.* As discussed earlier in this chapter, increasing positive stress at work can help to counteract negative stress at work. Suggest taking on assignments that meet your own long-term career development needs, as identified in Chapter 4, or to make your work more rewarding or meaningful. Enhancement of your own career is supported by the *Teacher Workload Study* (Pricewaterhouse-Coopers, 2001). Douglas (1996) describes ways that managers can increase eustress at work.

In general, managers will be much happier addressing the issue of stress if they can be seen to be working effectively with staff, rather than if they feel attacked or accused of causing too stressful an environment. Diplomacy is the key and, if you are in any doubt about your manager's perception of stress (for example if your manager seems very proud of his or her own high stress levels), practise your own stress management in private, not in public.

Step 4: Time to stop or time to go?

Whether you have burnout or rustout, overcoming the stress you are experiencing and developing positive stress at work will depend on how well your current position fulfils your needs. In evaluating this, some important questions to ask yourself are:

- Are there still career goals you would like to achieve or have your priorities changed?
- Does your current position hold opportunities to achieve the goals you currently have, or would you need to go somewhere else to achieve them?
- Would achievement of your goals require more training, or a career change?
- Does your current position provide opportunities to gain more training as part of your job or staff development?
- If you can accomplish steps towards achieving your goal, such as gaining valuable experience in your current position, what time limit would you put on completing this and moving on?
- Do you feel you can be happy in the long term working in the context of your workplace culture, as discussed in step 2, and under the supervision of your manager, as discussed in step 3?

3

STRESS IN
TEACHING

As early as the 1930s, stress was identified in teachers (Smith & Milstein, 1984). Travers and Cooper (1996) have documented the history of change in education since 1955 and its impact on teacher stress. Back in the 1980s, teachers reported experiencing work-related physical and mental strain, with stressors being lack of time, large classes, teaching workload and pupil misbehaviour (Trendall, 1989). In more recent years research results have expanded these stressors to include a greater number of pressures pulling teachers in many more different directions. Political stressors amounting to 'impossible expectations' were found in research with teachers in further education (Hartney, 2006). This chapter will look at three main sources of stress: the process of teaching; your identity as a teacher; and the politics of teaching.

The process of teaching

Regardless of other factors, the process of teaching is, in itself, quite stressful. As a teacher you are responsible not only for imparting knowledge to groups of children, but also for keeping them under control and for teaching them appropriate social behaviour. Even disregarding variations in the children's motivation, past social behaviour and prior learning, this would be a challenging task. However, often the children's backgrounds, lack of motivation and so on make the task of teaching even more stressful.

One aspect of the process of classroom teaching that is frequently cited as stressful by teachers is that of student discipline. This is hardly surprising as the role of teacher requires a balance between forming supportive relationships with your students so that they trust you enough to learn from you, and remaining in authority enough for you to prevent order in the classroom from breaking down. Complicating the issue is the multitude of past experiences of discipline the children have had. Parents, teachers and others have exerted control over each child you work with or, sometimes more problematically, they have neglected to do so. These past experiences of discipline lay the groundwork for your success or lack of success of maintaining control in the classroom, by setting up expectations within each child's mind of acceptable behaviour in themselves and in authority figures. Numerous studies, such as those conducted by Morton et al. (1997) and D. Lewis (1999), show the significance of classroom discipline in causing teachers stress.

Fortunately research has also identified ways of improving student discipline and many teachers have mastered this art and shared their strategies. Recent legislation also provides schools with more power to discipline students. Past research has shown that school approaches and policies can reduce teachers' stress (Hart et al., 1995). The Education and Inspection Act (2006), which provides a new statutory power for schools to discipline pupils, includes the responsibility of the school to have a behaviour policy. This can be developed with the involvement of staff, students and parents. According to the Act, students can be forcibly restrained when necessary, detentions can be used more flexibly and broadly, including weekend detentions, and parents have more responsibility for children's behaviour. Parenting orders and contracts may be used and parents must take greater responsibility for students who are excluded, with penalties and possible prosecution when students are found in public places during school hours without reason. Although focusing on the negative aspects of discipline, the protection of teachers provided by the Education and Inspection Act (2006) has the potential to greatly reduce the stress endured by teachers who have been subjected to verbal and physical abuse by students. More details of the Act are included in Further resources (page 149).

In terms of the approach taken by individual teachers, Hall et al. (1997) found that experienced teachers who were given training in human relations developed a more humanistic ideology to pupil control and experienced lower stress and a greater sense of being in control, when compared to a control group of similar teachers who did not receive the training. A more recent study showed that a profound improvement in the stressfulness of teacher-student relationships occurred when teachers were provided with consultation (Ray, 2007).

Admiraal et al. (2000) compared teachers who responded

actively to disruptive behaviour in the classroom with those who responded passively. Teachers who coped with classroom disruption with active coping styles, including raising the tension of interaction with the pupils and varying the intensity of activities, were more satisfied with the outcome than those who coped passively.

Having control over the curriculum has also been found to reduce teacher stress (Pearson & Moomaw, 2005). This can be really challenging, with more and more control being exerted centrally over what is taught and how it is taught. However, it is important that you maintain a sense of ownership over what you teach, and try to put your own 'spin' on it. Finally, the process of giving students feedback on their work can also be stressful (Stough & Emmer, 1998) and presenting feedback in terms of 'strengths' and 'action plan' reduces the challenges made by students, and the experience of stress in the teacher (Hartney, 2007).

Tips for low-stress teaching

- Familiarize yourself with your rights under the new Education and Inspection Act (2006), which you can access through the website listed in Further resources (page 149).
- If possible, get involved in developing your school's behaviour policy. At least know the policy, and follow it should behavioural problems arise. It is there to support you.
- Prevention is better than cure! Engage students in the material before they have a chance to become discouraged and misbehave.
- Incorporate the principles of human relations into your classroom management: recognize your students' needs for social relationships, strive to understand their motivations and encourage two-way communication.
- Respond actively and directly to misbehaviour. A passive approach will not prevent misbehaviour from escalating.
- Make use of consultation. Talk to other, more experienced, teachers who enjoy their work, a counsellor with knowledge of teaching issues or a coach, such as the free online coaching

provided by the Teacher Support Network at www.teacher-support.info.

- Control the content of what you teach, as much as possible. When the curriculum is strictly defined for you, personalize it by adding your own ideas, personal stories and interpretations.
- When giving students feedback on their work present positive feedback in terms of 'strengths' and negative feedback in terms of 'action plan'.

Your identity as a teacher

How you define yourself as a teacher, and how you believe others view teachers generally, has a great impact on your experience of stress. Unfortunately teachers report feeling undervalued and feel stressed by a lack of recognition and praise for the work that they do (Boyle et al., 1995; Brown et al., 2002) and by low public esteem (National Union of Teachers, 1999). Lack of status is a major predictor of job dissatisfaction in teachers (Travers & Cooper, 1993), and low status and poor pay are major sources of stress for teachers (Travers & Cooper, 1997). The feelings of being undervalued by society are obviously justified, although this is beginning to change with greater public recognition of the challenges teachers face, and more support being provided by new legislation and policies.

Although affected directly by social perceptions of teachers, teachers themselves often carry a negative view of teaching, which causes them great stress. Teachers report feelings of guilt (Brown et al., 2002), problems with 'self-efficacy', that is feeling competent and in control (Brouwers & Tomic, 2000; Friedman, 2000a), and teachers are frequently plagued with self-defeating beliefs about what constitutes being a good teacher (Chorney, 1998). The variations in teachers' internal perceptions of what it means to be a teacher makes the difference between those teachers who thrive, despite difficult circumstances, and those who feel overwhelmed and become burnt out.

Self-efficacy, the belief that you are a capable and competent teacher, is paramount to your avoidance of negative stress. Teachers with a greater sense of empowerment and professionalism have greater job satisfaction and lower stress (Pearson & Moomaw, 2005). Brouwers & Tomic's (2000) study explored the interplay between self-efficacy and all three components of burnout in teachers. Their research indicated that as teachers become emotionally exhausted, their self-efficacy is lowered. This in turn lowers the teachers' sense of personal accomplishment, and over time leads to depersonalization, and the cynical attitude towards others that accompanies it. Friedman (2000a) found that newly qualified teachers' self-efficacy worsened as they found they were unable to live up to their ideal performances. Initially teachers are highly idealistic and committed, but as reality sets in they may become frustrated and experience burnout. After this process of disillusionment teachers reach a crossroads, at which point they may adapt and continue on as teachers, or alternatively they may choose to abandon the profession. A recent online survey indicated that half of the teachers in the UK have considered leaving teaching (Fuller, 2007).

Despite the importance of developing a strong sense of self-efficacy, your perception of the control you have over the classroom environment needs to be realistic. Bibou-Nakou et al. (1999) explored the role of attributions in teachers. They presented teachers with hypothetical class management situations and found that those who blamed themselves for difficulties were also more vulnerable to stress, as indicated by symptoms of burnout. Therefore, it is important to keep a balance in your mind between those events that are under your control, and those that are not. Feeling 100 per cent responsible for everything that occurs in the classroom will set you up to feel like a failure, and to experience even greater stress.

Therefore, as well as keeping a healthy sense of being in control, it is important for you to have realistic expectations of yourself. Chorney (1998) looked at self-defeating beliefs in teachers, which were defined as those beliefs teachers have about being a good teacher that are unfounded by logical or empirical evidence, and have a strong likelihood of causing a teacher to have unrealistic expectations of their performance in the work environment. She found that the majority of teachers in the study evaluated their own value as teachers in absolute terms, such as: *'In order to be a good teacher, I believe that I must . . .'* or *'In order to be a good teacher, I believe that I need to . . .'* resulting in self-defeating beliefs, which were significantly associated with high levels of stress.

Self-efficacy has recently been shown to be significantly related to self-esteem in teachers (Huang & Liu, 2007). Juhasz (1990) argued that in the field of research, teacher self-esteem has been ignored in favour of student self-esteem. She suggested there are three teacher roles that form the basis of their professional self-esteem: the teacher as a facilitator of student learning; the teacher as a participant in planning policies and procedures; and the teacher as a developing professional. While other researchers have argued that the multiple roles of teachers are actually a source of stress (Pithers & Soden, 1998), Juhasz proposes that self-esteem is 'earned' through participation in these three roles. Self-esteem requires self-acceptance, which means you do not have to be the best at everything. As a teacher you can allow yourself to have a range of goals, from excelling in certain areas, to competence in others, to not even attempting others. This allows you to earn self-esteem through shifting priorities and self-expectations, while remaining realistic and true to your values and abilities.

Tips for developing your self-image as a teacher

- Take note of everything positive you hear or read about teachers or teaching. Do not negate any of it.
- Discuss with your colleagues the impact and potential impact of government changes that affect teaching, advocacy for the profession by others such as teachers' unions and associations and supportive reports in the media. The more you think and talk about positive moves in teaching, the more profoundly it will affect your self-image.
- Write down some affirmations about yourself as a teacher, and read them daily. Here are some examples:

55

> *'As a teacher, I deserve respect from myself, my students and society.'*
> *'As a teacher, I am doing one of the most important jobs imaginable.'*
> *'As an ethical and knowledgeable teacher, I can make a difference to many children's lives.'*
> *'Teachers provide the foundation for all academic and intellectual pursuits.'*
> *'I care deeply about children, and about the future. By teaching them, I am participating in shaping the future of the world.'*
> *'Today I will offer new skills, insights and wisdom to my students. It is their choice to accept this offer.'*

- Consider signing up for a daily affirmation email, such as the one provided by www.sunnythoughts.com.
- Actively take control in the classroom, and be aware that you are the most influential person present. Do not turn a blind eye to misbehaviour.
- Keep a realistic view of what is possible, and which factors are beyond your control. As long as you do your best, there is no reason to feel guilty about things you cannot change.
- Allow your self-esteem to be based on developing a range of competencies, without needing to excel at all of them. Give yourself credit for working towards goals, even if you have not yet achieved them.
- Seek support if you feel you have a negative view of yourself as a teacher or of teaching in general or if you recognize any of the symptoms of burnout in yourself (emotional exhaustion, lack of personal accomplishment or depersonalization). You can obtain teacher-specific support from the Teacher Support Line on 08000 562 561 in England and 08000 855 088 in Wales.

The politics of teaching

Teaching has always been tied up with politics, and the influence politics has on teaching is a major source of stress for teachers. Politics affect teachers within the power structures of individual schools, as well as on a national level. The management and structure of the school and lack of status and promotion are major predictors of job dissatisfaction in teachers (Travers & Cooper, 1993). Yet headteachers are not immune to stress themselves. Indeed, the great responsibility they carry for the students, staff and reputation of the school involves a greater number of stressors than straightforward teaching. The National Association of Headteachers (NAHT) reported on a survey involving 1,800 schools, which showed a rise in stress cases among headteachers and 38 per cent of all absence among heads being due to work-related stress, a rise of 26 per cent since the previous year (BBC News, 2005). Cooper and Kelly (1993) found that job dissatisfaction and mental ill health was higher in school headteachers than in principals and directors of further and higher education establishments. Female secondary headteachers had greater job dissatisfaction than men, while male headteachers suffered more mental ill health. The greatest sources of stress for senior teachers were work overload and handling relationships with staff. Another study detailed role overload leading to stress in senior teachers (Friedman, 2000b). In the UK, headteachers consistently work longer hours than other teachers and other professionals, even taking into account school holidays (PricewaterhouseCoopers, 2001).

Teachers have reported innovation and change in education as a considerable source of stress, particularly when the changes being made are perceived by the teachers as irrational, leaving them feeling powerless (Brown et al., 2002). Despite reporting a high level of satisfaction with their work, teachers are stressed by educational change and curriculum initiatives, especially when they contradict the teachers' own professional values (Moriarty et al., 2001).

Perhaps the greatest source of stress for teachers that has resulted from political change in the ways schools operate is school inspection. Brimblecombe and Ormston (1995) explored teachers' perceptions of the school inspection process and its impact on them before, during and after the inspection. Many teachers find the period before the inspection to be the most stressful time. This period begins when the teacher becomes aware of the scheduled inspection, with the stress increasing as the inspection draws near. The attitude of school leaders is paramount, with their support reducing stress in teachers and panic measures increasing stress, as panic gets passed down the line. In particular, attempts to 'clam' staff by warning them not to say anything that may reflect negatively on the school and last-minute changes to policies and schemes of work are extremely stress inducing to teachers. Ball (2003) described how teachers feel forced into acts of fabrication to present a more positive image of the school.

Recent changes in the way that Ofsted inspections are carried out should go a long way to alleviating teachers' stress. Ofsted explicitly state that schools are not required, or expected, to make any specific preparations for inspection. An online self-evaluation form (SEF) is provided for schools to keep continually updated, which forms the basis of the inspection. Inspectors will always study this carefully before visiting the school and do not require additional paperwork to be sent to them. Reporting and Analysis for Improvement through School Self-Evaluation (RAISEonline), the replacement for the Ofsted Performance and Assessment (PANDA) report and the DfES Pupil Achievement Tracker (PAT), makes it easier for schools to explore their available performance data in depth, down to individual pupil level, and to save and update copies with the latest local information.

Two days' notice is now given prior to an Ofsted inspection, which will last no longer than two days. Following the inspection, oral feedback will be given on the school's major strengths and weaknesses, and the report will be sent to the school to check for accuracy prior to publication on Ofsted's website at www.ofsted.gov.uk.

According to the Brimblecombe and Ormston (1995) study, more women, regardless of post, report worry at being observed during the inspection. Other studies have identified 'evaluation apprehension' as being pertinent to student teachers, and as becoming less stressful over time as positive experiences of observation occur (Capel, 1997; Morton et al., 1997). According to Jarvis (2002) there is a lack of research in this area with qualified teachers, although clearly there is overlap with the issue of school inspection. Brimblecombe and Ormston (1995) report that a balance is needed between presenting the school as it really is, and presenting the school in the best possible light. There is a tendency for teachers to plan lessons to be more didactic than usual when they know they are going to be observed, as they report feeling more in control of such lessons. Ironically, this typically puts nervous teachers under increased stress. Teachers report finding it very stressful awaiting the arrival of inspectors, and can also be stressed by the feeling that inspectors are observing them too much or too little. Rude or critical inspectors, while in the minority, can have a negative effect on the inspection as a whole. Mindful of this, Ofsted has introduced a code of conduct for inspectors, so this is unlikely to occur. However, nervousness can occasionally cause *teachers* to appear obstructive, hostile or resentful, resulting in a negative interchange with inspectors.

Brimblecombe and Ormston (1995) report that the time after the inspection has been completed can also be a time when the effects of stress are apparent. Many teachers value the opportunity to discuss observations with inspectors, although they do not always have this opportunity. Teachers may be stressed by formal feedback to large groups, or to the whole school, especially when they cannot challenge the judgements made by inspectors unless they are based on misinformation. Lack of anonymity is a concern in small schools, as each member of staff is identifiable. Teachers fear the effects of the Ofsted report on their career prospects, and do not want to be suspected of poor practice. Absenteeism is higher than normal in the week following an inspection and Brimblecombe and Ormston (1995) suggest that schools where a measured, proactive approach has been made towards inspection may be less likely to have staff illness afterwards.

Tips for dealing with politics in teaching

- Recognize the greater responsibility and stress that accompanies senior positions, particularly headteacher positions.
- If you feel stressed about an upcoming inspection, consider why. Is it fear of the unknown? Many teachers feel, with

hindsight, that they need not have been so stressed about the inspection.

- Get a clear view of the focus and purpose of the inspections, and try to develop a positive attitude to the process of change.
- Recognize the control you have over your part of the process, rather than feeling helpless.
- Think of your school inspection as a collaborative process. Treat inspectors with courtesy and respect, and expect the same from them.
- Give support to your colleagues – you are all in this together – and expect support from your managers. Talk to your union if you do not feel you are receiving adequate support. If you plan ahead as a team, you won't need to make last-minute changes.
- See the inspection as an opportunity to showcase what your school does well. If you can't think of anything, you are probably working in the wrong place!
- Practise relaxation skills, particularly when being observed.
- Take opportunities to debrief and learn from the inspection experience after it is over.

Do not:

- Hang on to the past or resist change. Instead, participate fully and help define the future you envision.
- Participate in group panic. You will think more clearly if you remain calm.
- Feel you need to hide anything from the inspectors. They may be able to give constructive feedback on areas of difficulty.
- Allow your resentment about the process to affect your interaction with other staff, students or inspectors.
- Treat the inspectors as the cause of any negative feelings you have – they are simply doing their jobs.

4

CAREER
DEVELOPMENT

There are many different reasons that teachers decide to teach, and some of them can be a source of stress in themselves. Therefore, it makes no sense to discuss stress in teachers as if teachers are all affected by the same kinds of professional issues. It is more useful to think of specific stresses that might be affecting subgroups of teachers. Some of the more common motivations for entering the education sector are reflected in the following five descriptions of different teachers below. You may recognize yourself and your colleagues immediately, you may find you do not fit clearly into one category or you may find that none of the categories applies to you. The descriptions are intended to illustrate some of the sources of stress arising from career-choice and career-development issues, and are certainly not intended to pigeonhole everyone!

The 'professional' teacher

For some, teaching is a vocation or a calling. Professional teachers go into teaching for all the right reasons. They know that they want to teach before entering the profession, and there are often altruistic reasons underlying their motivations. They may feel teaching is the best way for them to contribute to society, that they have specialized knowledge to share or simply that they want to be part of moulding the next generation. They may enjoy working with children and adolescents and find it fulfilling watching them gaining knowledge and competence. Professional teachers may have a passion for teaching, for learning or for their subject areas. They care deeply about their work.

Case study – the 'professional' teacher: Veronica

Veronica's own schooldays were the best days of her life. She admired her teachers, fitted in well and always wanted to teach. She had no problems with discipline and worked hard to earn good grades. She went into teacher training immediately after completing school and straight into primary school teaching after completing her BEd. She is very involved in her work and is always one step ahead of the academic routine. She is popular with the students, other teachers and administrators and is highly respected as a teacher. Despite her success at doing a job she has always believed in, Veronica has noticed a decline in educational standards since she started in teaching 30 years ago, and is concerned that many of her students are barely literate. Try as she might to encourage them, very few will read a book for pleasure. She feels that these days, students have no interest in developing understanding. Secretly, Veronica feels that the school administrators are more concerned with appearances than with what the students learn.

Stressors affecting professional teachers

- Professional teachers may lack respect for colleagues whom they feel are not truly committed to the job.
- They may have problems with management, feeling that the students' education is not always the top priority.
- They may feel unhappy that standards of education have deteriorated and feel their professionalism is being undermined by various political changes.
- They may feel unappreciated by students.
- They may feel constrained by regulations that have restricted what they teach and the way that they teach.

The 'manager-in-training'

Managers-in-training are teachers who work hard and have much to contribute to education. However, unlike professional teachers, their desire is to manage people rather than to teach. While they might be perfectly competent as teachers, they may be frustrated with their position in the educational system, and would far rather be running things than doing the hands-on, day-to-day teaching. They may be frustrated with the way that they are managed, particularly if they feel they would do a better job. Alternatively, they may get on very well with management, but be less well liked by other teachers. They may also become irritated with daily interactions with students, feeling the school rules are not taken seriously. For them, the smooth running of the school is more important than individual personal circumstances.

Case study – the 'manager-in-training': Jacob

Jacob worked hard at school and always had ambitions to be a manager. He completed his degree in business studies and was pleased to get a job teaching A level business studies at the local high school immediately afterwards, which he saw as a stepping stone to a management position at the school. Jacob's work is always well organized and his record keeping is impeccable. He always arrives early for classes and his students know that they must arrive on time, otherwise they will be in trouble. His classes are always well disciplined. In his 12 years of teaching Jacob has applied for several management positions in other schools, but has always had a hard time demonstrating that he has the required experience. When he was recently turned down for an internal management position at his own school, he was told that they could not possibly lose him from his current position.

Stressors affecting managers-in-training

- Managers-in-training may have conflicts with colleagues whom they feel are not following correct procedures.
- They may feel frustrated from a lack of recognition of their management skills.
- They may have problems with students making excuses for poor performance.
- While they have respect for the hierarchy of the school, they may be disliked by students and other teachers.
- They may struggle with others' perceptions of favouritism with management, but feel unappreciated in terms of rewards.
- They may alienate others with their enthusiasm for rules, regulations and Ofsted.

The 'fall-back' teacher

Fall-back teachers lived a previous life working in professions that they now teach. Sometimes they enjoyed their previous work far more than teaching, and hark back to their glory days of doing 'real work' in the 'real world'. Others found they could not cope with the requirements of their chosen vocation and decided not to continue to work in that industry. They may have been made redundant, been fired or chose to leave because they had burnt out, or for other reasons such as flexibility around childcare. In any case, the defining characteristic of the fall-back teacher is that they are identified with their original chosen career, not with teaching.

Case study – the 'fall-back' teacher: Leonard

Leonard loves to paint. He has always had a passion for art, doing well at art college, and going on to have a successful exhibition, during which he sold several pieces of art for considerable sums of money. Determined to make it as an artist, he took a voluntary position at an art gallery and spent several years without paid employment. During that time he sold a few more pieces of artwork, raising barely enough money to cover the cost of his materials. Eventually he was persuaded to take a PGCE course by the Benefits Service. This allowed him to get a job as an art teacher at his local secondary school, where he has worked for the past five years.

Stressors affecting fall-back teachers

- Fall-back teachers may continue to be bitterly disappointed at the failure of the career they loved.
- They may feel humiliated at their failure.
- They may lack motivation for teaching.
- They may have problems with job-related skills, such as administration or getting along with others, which may have lead to their previous downfall.
- They may alienate others by acting in a superior way.

- They may have ambivalent feelings about their students' successes.

The 'day-job' teacher

Day-job teachers are similar to fall-back teachers, in that they identify with the profession that they teach, rather than with teaching per se. The difference between the day-job teacher and the fall-back teacher is that day-job teachers are actively involved in working towards their alternative careers, or have ambitions to do so in the future. As with all the other types, day-job teachers may be extremely competent as teachers, and may even be more talented as teachers than they would be in their chosen professions. However, for them, teaching is a compromise, and they would prefer to be making their living full time in the industry of their choice. A variation on the day-job teacher is the part-time professional teacher. These teachers have limited or considerable success in the career of their choice, but choose to teach part time, either to supplement their income, or to contribute to the next generation.

Case study – the 'day-job' teacher: Ron

Ron always dreamed of making it as a musician. He disliked school and, ironically, he hated music lessons in particular. He never learned to read music or play an instrument during his schooldays, preferring instead to listen to his vast record collection at home. At university he avoided attending lectures by teaching himself the guitar, and soon set up a rock band with a group of other students. After graduating with a passing grade in combined studies, and a blissful summer touring college campuses and student venues, he drifted from low-paid job to unemployment. His college band broke up, as his former band members moved on to professional careers. Ron was able to start a new band with a group of young unemployed men, and played gigs in local pubs and clubs every weekend. He started in teaching with some private English tuition, and found it much better paid than shop work. He took a TEFL course and, after a year of travelling and teaching, continued to work part time teaching English in a private school for foreign students as he struggled to form a new band and try and make it in the music industry. He continues to work part time teaching English, while working on music unpaid on his days off. Popular with his students, he is understanding of their problems, and able to motivate them to express themselves through language. However, his students see him more as a friend than an authority figure, and for this reason he has ongoing frustrations with the school over the lateness and poor attendance of his students.

Stressors affecting day-job teachers

- Day-job teachers may be exhausted by the amount of work they are doing if they are also pursuing other career ambitions.
- They may be relatively uncommitted to teaching.
- They may have problems with job-related skills, such as administration or getting along with others, that are making it difficult for them to succeed in their chosen career.
- They may alienate others by acting in a superior way.
- They may feel humiliated at their lack of success in their chosen career.
- They may feel 'stuck' in teaching.
- They may have ambivalent feelings about their students' successes.

The 'undefined career' teacher

Undefined career teachers, like many other teachers, are primarily involved in education because it is a job they can do, rather than one they choose to do. Unlike many of the others affected by this issue, there is no alternative career that they would prefer to be involved in, yet they have no particular passion for teaching either. They may have studied academic subjects that do not have a career path connected to them, or they may have had interests that were quite general. Although undefined career teachers may suffer from relatively little stress related to career choice, because there is nothing else they would rather be doing, they may feel rather disconnected from their work.

Case study – the 'undefined career' teacher: Rebecca

Rebecca enjoyed school and university and always got on well with everyone. After graduating, she had no idea what she wanted to do. She moved back in with her parents and started work as a waitress at a local pub. The hours were long and antisocial so she was pleased when two years later she landed a 9–5 job at a local bank. However, she found the work boring and the holidays few and far between, so she looked around for something else for four years. When a friend of hers completed a PGCE and became a teacher Rebecca followed suit, looking forward to the long academic holidays a career in teaching would provide. She immediately got a job teaching maths at her local secondary school. She enjoyed the work more than she had working at the bank, as she was able to interact with others more, and the hours and the pay were much better than the pub. The money she was on was good enough for her to pay off her student loans and get her own flat. She sees no reason to change anything about her life, but sometimes feels she should be more enthusiastic about her work.

Stressors affecting undefined career teachers

- Undefined career teachers may feel a lack of commitment to their work.
- They may feel disappointed in their lack of direction and ambition.
- They may feel inferior to 'professional' teachers.
- They may find their work boring.

Self-reflection: what kind of teacher are you?

Think about the case studies. Ask yourself the following questions:

What were the reasons I chose to teach initially?
- Do I have a passion for teaching and learning?
- Do I have a passion for my subject area?
- Is there another career I would rather be doing?
- Do I care about my work?
- Do I care about my students?
- Is this the best place for me to be working right now?

Our personal career goals: a source of stress

As we have seen there are many stressors that affect teachers, related to career choices as well as to teaching itself. Unresolved feelings about these career choices may be causing you more stress than you realize and by avoiding facing these feelings you are bottling up the stress and making it worse. The solution is to take a long, hard look at your life situation and to decide, honestly, what you really want from your career. You also need to be honest with yourself about what would be required to make it in your chosen career. What has prevented you from doing so in the past? Skills, abilities, confidence? If you did not have those things in the past, will you really be able to get them in the future? Only you can answer these questions, although it may help to do a little background research to find out some of the answers.

You can find out more about what your key personal strengths are by taking the VIA Inventory of Strengths, available online at www.viastrengths.org, or for a really detailed assessment of your strengths and personality, try www.personality-strengths.com. When you view the results of the assessment, think carefully about your key strengths. Will your chosen career allow you to maximize these strengths or will you be frustrated or stressed by having to work in areas of weakness and having to suppress your true values and abilities?

Directing energy towards goal achievement

It may be that teaching is right for you, no matter how you got into it. If this is the case, hanging on to what might have been is only draining your energy and it may be time to let go of the past and accept your role as a teacher. If this is not the case, and you feel you really would be much happier in another job (and that job is realistically within your abilities and current life situation), then it may be time to focus on directing your energy towards making that fantasy job into a reality. That will require more energy expenditure on your part, but you will not be wasting your energy and causing yourself stress by trying to suppress your feelings of dissatisfaction.

Self-promotion

A major aspect of making career changes is self-promotion, which can be an incredible source of stress for many people. A lucky few are born with an innate ability to promote themselves. From an early age, they are able to describe their achievements and personal qualities with an astounding level of self-belief. Often so much so, that occasionally it can be difficult for both the employer and the employee when their mediocre abilities become apparent! Yet other perfectly competent individuals have the opposite problem, and seem unable to talk about their abilities without feeling deceitful or arrogant. Who turns out to be a natural self-promoter, and who does not, probably depends on many factors, such as past experiences, family and culture. Whatever the reason, people who find self-promotion difficult are likely to experience much more stress when it comes to applying for jobs and promotions than those who do not.

Failure versus feedback

There is a saying (that has been attributed to several authors and prominent figures): 'There is no failure, only feedback.' What this means is that when you are unsuccessful, you have a choice in how you interpret the outcome. You can choose to interpret that outcome as a failure, which leads to a negative evaluation of yourself, your performance and your ability to perform in the future. Alternatively, you can glean information from how you performed to help you perform better in the future. By looking at the result of your performance as feedback you can recognize what you did well, rather than simply focusing on what didn't work. That way, you can feel good about being part-way to accomplishing your goal. More importantly, you retain the motivation to try again next time.

This is the opposite of what psychologists call 'learned helplessness'. The idea of learned helplessness came out of research carried out with dogs, which showed that, when a dog was caged then put under stress, after a while it would simply give up and accept the stress. Later, the dog would continue to passively receive the stress, even when its cage was opened and it was free to leave. People have also been found to develop learned helplessness (Hiroto & Seligman, 1975), at times refusing to recognize they are able to change their situations simply because they did not have the power to do so at an earlier time. This also relates to research by Judge & Locke (1993), who found that people who feel dependent on others for their self-worth, who are perfectionists about their own work and who generalize from single events (for example, thinking doing one thing wrong means they are a bad person), have lower job satisfaction and higher levels of depression. It is important, then, to maintain a sense of balance between having high standards and being gentle with yourself in striving to reach those standards. Seeing success as a process requiring learning and adaptation can greatly assist with this.

Knowing when to stop

There is a time in every working person's career development when they reach the optimal position for their talents, energy and stress-management skills. Sadly, many people never reach their optimal position, through lack of opportunity or education. However, equally sadly, others actually do reach their potential then spoil things by moving beyond that level, resulting in stress.

Often a promotion will not result in substantially more money, but will result in substantially more stress. The catch-22 is that they do not feel able to move backwards without losing face and feeling they have failed. Being happy in your career includes the ability to know when you are really happy in your job and, when you know you are functioning optimally, stopping there.

Knowing when to go

It may take many different jobs to find the job that is right for you, the job that will make you happy in your work. It is always stressful leaving and going somewhere new, but if you are really unhappy where you are you may be better off facing up to the fact that the situation is not going to change. Move on to somewhere that might meet your needs, rather than resigning yourself to a lifetime of stress. The questions listed at the end of Chapter 2 may help you to evaluate whether this is the case for you.

Introduction

Work relationships are so important to the management of stress at work that this entire chapter is devoted to managing stress resulting from relationships at work. Taris et al. (2004) distinguish between three types of work relationships that teachers may experience as sources of stress: relationships with students, relationships with colleagues and the teacher's relationship with the organization itself. They found statistical support for these distinctions in terms of stress and also found that problems in each of these kinds of relationship lead to withdrawal from that specific type of relationship, although not necessarily from the others. Therefore, relationships with students and relationships with colleagues will both be addressed in this chapter. As mentioned in Chapter 1, the focus of the book is dealing with issues over which the individual teacher has influence and thus we will not address the teacher's relationship with the organization here.

Reciprocity

Work relationships and communication are complex and there is much literature relating to how they may both be a source of stress. According to Edelmann (1993), satisfaction in work relationships is based on reciprocity. Conflicts occur between colleagues when help and support with shared tasks is not given and received equally. Therefore, failure to accept a fair share of the workload or to take responsibility for shared tasks may be a source of conflict in relationships with colleagues. This is consistent with recent findings related to 'equity' in work relationships (Taris et al., 2004), which show the need for a balance between what people 'invest' in a work relationship (for example, time, skills or effort) and the benefits they receive (for example, status, pay or appreciation).

Research by Van Horn et al. (2001) explored reciprocity in relationships among teachers and between teachers and their students. They found that teachers reported perceiving significantly more investments than outcomes, which was related to their experience of stress and burnout. Teachers who invest more than they receive in relationships with colleagues experience significantly more stress due to tensions in these relationships, and are more likely to experience the emotional exhaustion symptom of burnout. Interestingly, teachers who invest more than they benefit from their relationships with their students experience more stress from interactions with students, and also from time pressure and aspects directly related to teaching, such as poor equipment. They are more likely to experience all three symptoms of burnout: emotional exhaustion, depersonalization and lack of personal accomplishment.

Developing reciprocal relationships with colleagues

- *Reciprocal relationships are based on give and take.* Try to ensure you give and receive help and support in roughly equal measures.
- *Notice when people are reciprocating.* Teachers cannot *all* be giving more than they receive from each other! Notice when your colleagues invest effort in their relationships with you, and when they express appreciation or offer you support. Do not discount the positive aspects of these relationships.
- *We all have problems with giving and/or taking.* Recognize that successful professionals always have a team of helpers supporting them in one way or another. You don't have to do it all alone.
- *Giving support.* Respond to both direct and indirect requests for help. If a colleague is struggling with a task you find easy, and you have time, politely offer to help.
- *Receiving support.* If a colleague is particularly skilled or knowledgeable about something you find difficult but have to do as part of your job, ask for help directly, in a way that acknowledges their skills and generosity.
- *Remember your manners.* Say 'please' beforehand, 'thank you' afterwards and openly acknowledge their competence and help if the matter comes up later. If you have helped someone else, be gracious. Say 'you're welcome' if they thank you.
- *Avoid asking for help with a task a colleague finds difficult or*

unpleasant. The mix of personalities is such that there often will be someone who would gladly help, but it is better to brazen it out yourself if it is a job everyone loathes.

- *Even it out*. Don't always ask for or provide help to the same people. Make a point of giving help to and receiving help from people you do not like. This will develop your reputation as a good team player. It also reduces the development of 'cliques' at work, which can be a precursor to inadvertent bullying.

Bakker et al.'s (2000) research with teachers showed that depression and burnout are different experiences, and that they are related to different kinds of relationship problems. While depression is associated with a lack of reciprocity in intimate relationships, burnout is associated with a lack of reciprocity in relationships with students. The amount of stress teachers are under also predicts the number of negative relationship they have with pupils. Teachers who experience high levels of stress may exhibit anger and hostility in their interactions with students, causing more negative relationships and in turn, more stress (Yoon, 2002).

Bakker et al.'s (2000) research describes how equity theory relates to the teacher's role. Although the relationship between student and teacher may seem unequal on the surface, with the teacher in the role of provider of knowledge and the student in the role of recipient, the teacher has certain expectations of what the student might give in return. These expectations might include deference, gratitude, enthusiasm and effort. When students are inattentive, disrespectful or bored, the teacher's efforts are not being reciprocated. Burnout occurs when this becomes a chronic, ongoing situation, with the teacher continually giving more than they receive. Van Horn et al.'s (1999) research has shown how this pattern affects teachers.

Developing reciprocal relationships with students

Giving
- Always include time for questions and answers either before, during or after teaching sessions.

- Make time for students to see you individually.
- Make it clear you want to help your students to do well, using phrases such as: *'Let me know if you are having difficulty, and I'll try and help.'*
- Refer students to support services where appropriate, such as counselling, housing, disability services, librarians and so on. With the *Every Child Matters* initiative, you have a responsibility to support the whole child, not just their learning.

Receiving

- Role-model the language and behaviour you would like from the students. Always say 'please', 'thank you' and 'you're welcome' to students, and give them your full attention when they are speaking.
- If you are struggling physically, for example if you have your hands full, ask a student for help if no one offers: *'Could you hold the door open for me, please.'*
- Ask students to help with minor tasks, such as distributing handouts, opening/closing windows and so on.
- Make behavioural expectations clear to students, for example: *'Please don't talk while someone else is speaking,'* or *'Please bring your assignment preparation to next week's session.'*
- If you have helped a student who does not acknowledge your help, ask for feedback, for example: *'Does that help?'* or *'Is that useful?'* This usually prompts a courteous response.

Relationship rules

Edelmann (1993) describes a major source of conflict as being concerned with how well colleagues adhere to 'relationship rules', a set of informal rules that are commonly accepted in the work context. General rules between all work colleagues are: rules of support, for example helping a colleague with a work-related task if a reasonable request is made; rules of intimacy, for example respecting colleagues' privacy; third-party rules, for example not criticizing a colleague in public; and task-related rules concerning the fulfilment of specific tasks, for example planning lessons or assigning work to students. Keeping these relationship rules helps to ensure the smooth running of the workplace, while breaking the rules may lead to conflict between colleagues.

Although Edelmann's (1993) rules may widely apply to the way people would like to be treated at work, the actual adherence to these rules in practice is highly variable. Although relationship rules are based on common understanding, because the rules are not explicitly communicated or formally taught, awareness of these rules is likely to depend largely on individuals' general social skills. It may even be accepted within a subgroup's work culture that certain relationship rules are not adhered to. Examples of this may be when teachers decline to 'take on' any additional tasks that they perceive as taking time away from teaching, thus not taking their fair share of non-teaching tasks (although according to the *National Agreement*, all teachers should be declining inappropriate administrative tasks), or support staff who feel overworked complaining about or criticizing colleagues to third parties to relieve their frustration. Such behaviours may even be condoned within groups or organizations. This idea is supported by Cooper and Cartwright (2004), who point out that the extent to which positive or negative behaviours are tolerated depends on the culture of the organization and the attitudes and awareness of management. A vicious cycle emerges, as Taris et al. (2004) argue that one way of coping with inequity in work relationships is to develop negative attitudes towards students, colleagues or the organization. With these issues being inherent in the workplace it is no wonder staff experience burnout, as negative attitudes about others is actually a symptom (see Chapter 1).

Relationship rules with colleagues

- *Be friendly*. This includes greetings, eye contact, smiles of acknowledgement and so on.
- *Express mild personal interest*. Appropriate questions and comments include:

- *'How are you?'*
- *'How is your partner/children?'* (Use their names, and only ask if you have personally met the family members concerned.)
- *'Have a good weekend/holiday.'*
- *'You look very nice today.'*
- Avoid questions or comments implying intimacy such as:
    - Any specific comment on personal appearance, even if you consider it complimentary, for example *'Have you lost weight?'*
    - Specific questions about health or family problems.
    - Overt sexual flirtation.
    - The old adage, never discuss religion or politics (unless you teach religion/politics, in which case, do so carefully and tactfully).
- *Never gossip about colleagues* (no matter how fascinating they are, or how much you dislike them).
- *Never undermine a colleague, especially when they are not present.* Defend them in some way (even if you do not agree with their behaviour) if others criticize them.
- *Acknowledge the value of colleagues' ideas/contributions* (even if poorly expressed).
- *Rise above feelings of envy, competitiveness or distaste,* by recognizing your colleague has problems too.
- *Be a good sport if your colleague receives undue praise, favouritism or promotion.* Any other reaction will make you look petty or spiteful.

You also have relationship rules with students, although teachers vary in how important they consider these to be. Recognize that your students are almost always in a less powerful position than you are, as their teacher, and sometimes breaking relationship rules when they know you cannot is the only way they can get any sense of power in the relationship. This situation can be eased by showing your students respect, empowering them through appropriate teaching methods and adhering to appropriate relationship rules.

Relationship rules with students

- *Good timekeeping.* Arrive early, state when the class will begin/ end.
- *Give breaks* if the class is more than one hour.
- *Be courteous.* This will encourage the same from the students.
- *Encourage and reward self-discipline* rather than dependency on you to discipline their behaviour.
- *Do not express your feelings directly to students.* If you are very angry, make an appointment to see them later, when you can address the issue calmly.
- *Give yourself time to respond to difficult questions appropriately.* Breathe out fully and take a breath in before responding. Stay rational and do not get caught up in the heat of the moment.
- *Be willing to give students support.* If a student requests more help than is reasonable, focus on tips for self-sufficiency.
- *Never flirt overtly with students.* Always give gentle but clear messages of unavailability to any expressions of romantic or sexual interest from students. It is not unusual for students to develop strong feelings towards teachers, or to feel they can gain an advantage from an illicit relationship with a teacher. Taking advantage of this is an abuse of power, even when students are not 'under age'.
- *Treat students fairly and equally regardless of whom you like or dislike.* If you offer one student extra time or help, you should be willing to give the same individual attention to all students.
- *Develop a zero-tolerance attitude to disrespectful behaviour,* such as swearing, name-calling and aggression. However flexible and accepting you want to seem to your students, they will have more respect for you, for each other and for themselves, and you will create a safer environment if the classroom is a place where bad behaviour is not tolerated. However, do not overreact either. Respond directly, in a way that is appropriate and meaningful to the disrespectful students and onlookers.

Power plays

More extreme forms of relationship rule breaking include 'power plays' (Steiner, 1981). Power plays include attempts to control, exploit and manipulate others; overt and psychological threats; and harassment. Steiner (1981) argues that all power plays are difficult to handle, as fighting back typically leads to more unpleasantness. A difficulty specific to teachers that may arise as a result of relationship rule breaking is when one teacher uses individual students or groups of students to damage the reputation of other teachers, either among the student body or in order to encourage students to make complaints about the targeted teacher. Such power plays may be subtle or more overt harassment or bullying and as Cooper and Cartwright (2004) argue, may be tolerated in some work contexts.

Power plays can come from unlikely sources. The role of support staff, for example, has changed radically over the last few decades and it is not unusual to come across support staff who consider it beneath them to fulfil quite basic tasks such as photocopying, taking telephone messages and typing documents. Younger, female teachers in particular may be on the receiving end of power plays as blatant as 'Do it yourself!' when they request such support. This is unacceptable and the *National Agreement* specifies tasks that teachers have the right to refuse to carry out, which are detailed on pages 31–2.

Power plays are also common between colleagues at a similar level within an organization. This may be due to competitiveness, envy or feeling threatened. Again, younger women often receive power plays from older women, although it should be noted that men, women, older, younger, white and ethnic minority teachers can all be made to feel disadvantaged by these characteristics, and equally people of all demographic groups are capable of resorting to power plays and bullying. Such power plays can often include patronizing, condescending behaviour such as using the phrase 'With all due respect ...' before harshly criticizing an idea or suggestion, failing to pass on essential information, a variety of verbal and non-verbal put-downs and creating extra non-essential work for a colleague. Recipients of

81

power plays may be frustrated further by accusations of having no sense of humour, being too 'formal' or being 'unprofessional', depending on their response to such humiliations.

Power plays from colleagues

- *Control your feelings about colleagues who indulge in power plays and bullying.* They are not worth your energy, and it contributes nothing to your situation to 'hate' them.
- *Do not respond in kind when someone pulls a power play on you.* Doing so will only make you look as petty as them, whereas a gracious response makes you appear superior.
- *Defend others when you witness a power play,* focusing on the validity of the victim's position rather than their vulnerability.
- *Open up your colleagues' opinions if you are criticized in public.* Acknowledge the other person's 'point of view', then suggest: *'Let's see what other people think.'* This allows people to come to your defence and dilutes the effect of the power play. If no one comes to your defence, you might want to reconsider your point of view or your choice of workplace.
- *Check your facts if you think you are being made to do an unrealistic piece of work,* such as masses of complicated calculations. Often support staff can be as valuable for this as your line manager, but if you think a job is unreasonable ask your line manager for a discussion about the feasibility of completing the task within the specified timescale. You may be offered an extension, extra help or find that you didn't need to do all that work after all. Of course, you should have already checked it is not on the list of tasks you do not have to do, specified in the *National Agreement*.
- *Chase people up if they have said they will get back to you and do not within a week.* A brief, friendly note or email, stating the date and specifying the time you have been waiting will often work.

A variety of power plays can be used by students, ranging from the subtle to the overt. The most basic power plays can result from a deliberate failure to observe the relationship rules expected of them, such as arriving on time, staying seated and remaining quiet while the teacher or another student is speaking. More overt power plays include direct criticism of the teacher or other students, use of inappropriate or foul language and mocking the teacher or other students. Sometimes covert techniques can be used, such as making false accusations against a disliked teacher.

As school teachers have increasingly lost the power and skills to discipline pupils in the classroom, such power plays have become commonplace. However, Ofsted (2006) reported that behaviour in schools has improved lately, with almost all schools inspected having satisfactory pupil behaviour. Recent changes in legislation also give teachers more powers to discipline, with the introduction of the Education and Inspections Act (2006), but teachers do not necessarily have the skills to do so effectively. Worry about having more responsibility to discipline may cause more stress for teachers.

In addition, students with psychological problems such as attentional disorders and learning disorders, who previously may not have had access to mainstream education, may be participating in the educational process but have little control over their behavioural difficulties. Nevertheless it is important to remember that, although disabled, such students are capable of learning appropriate behaviour, and no teacher deserves to be treated disrespectfully at work. In circumstances where a disability is known, an open approach involving student support services may be the most effective. When a disability is evident but not known the most effective approach is to provide clear, consistent guidelines on acceptable behaviour and to report or document all incidents. According to the Education and Inspections Act (2006), schools are required to develop a discipline policy, which must be communicated to students and parents so all will be aware of expected behaviour.

Power plays from students

- *Control your feelings about students who indulge in power plays and bullying.* Recognize that they are learning social skills and the rules of appropriate behaviour and may not have learned these skills at home or school in the past.

- *Ignore or laugh off petty power plays when they do not merit your attention,* for example if a student makes a silly joke at your expense.
- *Pause mid-sentence and look directly at the student if they speak while you are trying to teach.* This will usually cause them to stop. If not, keep watching them until they are encouraged to be quiet by their peers, which will give you the support of the majority.
- *Open up ideas to the whole group if a student criticizes an idea or theory you have been presenting.* Either correct them if they are simply wrong, saying something like *'I think you have misunderstood the concept,'* or in the case of opinion, acknowledge the student's 'point of view', then suggest: *'Let's see what other people think'.* This allows the other students to come to your defence, and dilutes the effect of the power play. If they all share the challenging opinion, point out that the accepted view in your discipline is the one you presented, even though the student's comment may be a valid criticism.
- *Remain in authority.* Refer to policies and procedures if students try to manipulate you. For example follow through on giving detention, rather than using it as an empty threat.

Bullying

Additional sources of conflict between colleagues identified by Edelmann (1993) may be the result of individuals being excluded from subgroups or cliques, demographic differences, in particular age and gender, and personality clashes. In addition, misperceptions and misunderstandings may also cause conflict. These can all form the basis of workplace bullying.

Bullying is one stressor related to work relationships that has been well researched in recent years. Agervold and Mikkelsen (2004) reviewed a variety of estimates of the prevalence of bullying in the workplace, which ranged anywhere from 1–50 per cent of employees. According to Bully Online, at 20 per cent (of over 10,000 cases), teachers formed the largest group of callers to the now discontinued UK National Workplace Bullying

Advice Line. Agervold & Mikkelsen (2004) defined bullying as a negative and aggressive form of verbal or non-verbal communication, which is experienced as a threat to the victim's self-esteem, personality or professional competence, and which typically occurs over an extended period of time. In contrast, harassment may be short in duration and extremely intense, although the term harassment can also refer to bullying (Bjorkqvist et al., 1994). However, as Cooper and Cartwright (2004) argue, harassment and bullying exist on a continuum, with the more subtle and common forms at one extreme and physical aggression and bullying at the other, thus making it difficult to accurately define, evaluate and address.

Workplace bullying has been found to be a major stress factor for both victims and witnesses (Bjorkqvist et al., 1994). Employees who are bullied report significantly more stress, burnout, psychosomatic symptoms and time off sick than colleagues who have not been bullied at work (Agervold & Mikkelsen, 2004), and this research also shows that management style can directly or indirectly contribute to a higher level of bullying. This may be related to responses from supervisors or counsellors to reports of bullying from employees that cause the victim further harm (Ferris, 2004). For example unhelpful responses range from deeming the bullying behaviour appropriate, to equally attributing the behaviour to both parties as a 'personality conflict'. Furthermore, managers may actually be responsible for much of workplace bullying (Sparks et al., 2001). The withholding of information needed for an employee to effectively carry out his or her job may in itself constitute bullying (Agervold & Mikkelsen, 2004).

While management might seem a useful source of support, Ferris (2004) warned that there are two common responses to employees seeking support from the organization when they have been bullied and harassed, which are unhelpful or may lead to further problems. These responses are first that the bullying behaviour is deemed acceptable, and second that the bullying behaviour is considered attributable to both parties, and is described as a personality conflict. Ferris (2004) suggested that the injured party should consider whether it is worth approaching the organization for help at all, and whether a more useful strategy would be to become 'situationally passive' until another opportunity is found. Furthermore, she advised against entering into mediation as a potential solution in cases where the bully has targeted others (serial bullying); in cases where there is a power imbalance such as bullying occurring between a supervisor and an employee; and in cases where the victim has suffered a severe traumatic response, for example depression or anxiety. In these types of situations, Ferris (2004) argued, mediation may lead to further traumatization. Therefore, carefully consider the possible responses and related consequences before approaching management to resolve a complaint of harassment or bullying. However managers can be tremendously supportive and the National Association of Headteachers (2000) has produced guidelines on the prevention and management of bullying of both pupils and staff, which, if implemented, are extremely helpful.

One approach teachers use to manage the stress caused by difficult relationships at work is that of avoidance strategies, including techniques such as avoiding being alone with the bully and avoiding engaging in debate with the bully (R. Lewis, 1999). While withdrawal is a common response to perceived inequalities in work relationships, it should be noted that it is a key component of burnout (Taris et al., 2004), and thus the desire to withdraw may be an indication of stress-related problems rather than an effective strategy for stress management. Taris et al.'s (2004) research shows that in unequal relationships withdrawal in response to difficult behaviour actually reduces the quality of the relationship further, rather than balancing it, as both parties involved invest less and less in the relationship.

Further, Cooper and Cartwright (2004) argue that avoidance tactics are time-consuming and stressful, and instead advocate several strategies for changing the dynamics of a difficult relationship with a colleague or superior. These include: recognition of the problem and its effects; documentation of interactions between the parties involved; examination of the employer's policy and procedures for dealing with the problem; reporting the problem to either one's manager or human resources, depending on expected outcome; seeking clarification, information and resources from one's manager; gaining insight into one's own behaviour by asking for feedback from colleagues; and, finally, altering one's own behaviour. Whether to avoid the difficult person or attempt to change the relationship depends on the individual situation and, in particular, the support of management as detailed above. If the workplace culture is proactive and supportive, change would be the best option in the long term. However, if the workplace culture tolerates bullying, harassment and other stressors likely to lead to burnout, avoidance coupled with seeking opportunities elsewhere may be more productive.

Bullying by colleagues

- *Use body language to regain the upper hand.* Avoid defensive gestures such as arm folding. Instead of direct eye contact, look at the space in the middle of the forehead, just above the eyebrows. This is known as the 'business gaze' and is effective when dealing with bullies (Clayton, 2003).
- *Use assertive, passive or indirect behaviours,* depending on the situation (see Chapter 6).
- *Do not allow bullying to affect your self-esteem* or your view of your own personality or competence. Never comply with the poor image a bully may be presenting of you. Balance negative impacts on your sense of self by spending time with and talking to people who like and respect you.
- *Try to learn from the experience.* Look at the skills or characteristics the bully picks on to identify areas of your skills set to work on in the future. You can even address this openly and directly by asking for support in attending a training course.
- *Report any unambiguously inappropriate behaviour,* such as any threats, racial or sexual harassment or abuse, or physical violence, immediately.

As with milder power plays, bullying and harassment may also come from students. This can be extremely undermining to a teacher's self-confidence but, as with colleagues, there are techniques that can help.

Bullying by students

- *Use body language to regain the upper hand.* As with bullying colleagues, avoid defensive gestures such as arm folding. Instead of direct eye contact, look at the space in the middle of the forehead, just above the eyebrows. This is known as the 'business gaze' and is effective when dealing with bullies (Clayton, 2003).
- *Stay in authority.* Always remember that in your classroom, you are in charge. Become aware of, and consistently adhere to, the school's discipline policy. If necessary, ask the student to leave.
- *Control interruptions.* If a student is talking while you or another student are speaking, pause and look directly at the student. This may be enough to make them stop. If not, simply say: '*Can you listen while someone is/I am talking? You can go next.*' When you or the other student has finished, be sure to come back to the rude student, asking, '*What was it you wanted to say?*'
- *Keep badly behaved students behind.* After the class, tell them directly what it was about their behaviour that was a problem, and what they need to do to correct it. Explain that you cannot have disruption in your class, and you will have to take further action if it happens again. Be sure to follow up with further action if bad behaviour continues.
- *Tell someone, even if they are not in authority, about any difficult students immediately after the incident.* You may find others have experienced the same thing, and it helps verify your side of the situation if the problem escalates.
- *Report any inappropriate behaviour,* such as any threats, racial or sexual harassment, or physical violence, immediately.

6

DEALING WITH DIFFICULT PEOPLE

Personalities versus behaviours

In dealing with difficult people you should always be aware of the distinction between people's personalities and their behaviours. People's personalities are internally based, and are stable, so they do not change much over time (although stress can influence how aspects of their personalities are expressed). In contrast, people's behaviours are their actions in the world, and can be changed and controlled (although they are often the outward expression of internal issues of personality). Therefore, it is important that you focus on behaviours when you are thinking about change. Behaviours also improve greatly with competence so giving positive feedback for the behaviours you want, whether directly or indirectly, will encourage others (and ourselves) to engage in more positive behaviours.

When you are thinking about difficult people, you should remember that everyone starts out in life thinking of themselves as normal, and everyone notices other people's differences in comparison to themselves. It is helpful to question whether someone you are having a hard time with is really being difficult or whether they are just being different. A person might communicate differently, more quietly or loudly, more flamboyantly or placidly than you are used to. Take care not to pigeonhole people too quickly, as they may not be difficult at all!

Behaviours and styles of communication

Theorists on assertiveness have identified four major groupings of behaviour and communication style you may come across at work (Dickson, 1982; Stubbs, 1985; Rees & Graham, 1991). In this book, I will refer to these groupings as aggressive, assertive, passive and indirect. In general, aggressive, passive and indirect communication should be avoided in favour of assertive communication, although there are times when passive or indirect communication may be more appropriate or effective. Aggressive communication rarely wins you friends or influences people other than to make them think you are a bully.

Aggressive

Aggressive communication is exactly that, communication that expresses anger towards the listener, and often (but not always) bypasses important courtesies such as listening to and considering the other person's point of view, talking in a pleasant tone of voice and use of 'please', 'thank you' and the oft-neglected 'you're welcome'. Aggressive behaviours, such as banging doors, desk drawers, telephones and so on, sighing loudly and repeatedly and stomping feet when walking, also communicate anger. Very occasionally people use a loud tone and angry manner all the time, without meaning to or even being conscious of it, and some cultures are more comfortable with such behaviours than others. While for some aggression is a bad habit, and may reflect underlying personality issues, everyone has bad moods at one time or another, and tends to become more aggressive in their communication.

Assertive

Assertive communication is direct, to the point and respectful. Assertive communication involves listening to the other person's point of view and expressing your own point of view without dominating or submitting to the other person. Assertive communication is considered positive because it respects your own rights and responsibilities as well as the other person's. When you communicate assertively you focus on the present, and current, relevant matters in hand and not past frustrations or difficulties.

Passive

Passive communication involves habitually deferring to the other person. Passive communication implies a judgement that the other person's point of view is more valid and important than your own. Some people use passive communication because they are in a state of learned helplessness, in which case they can learn to communicate in other ways, which show more respect for themselves. You may also use passive communication to avoid conflict with a bully and in this case it may be strategic, as long as it does not become long term, and lead to learned helplessness. In other cases use of passive communication may indicate underlying personality issues or a lack of original ideas. Some people who passively communicate are simply too lazy to come up with or express their own points of view.

Indirect

The fourth type of communication I refer to as indirect communication. Other authors have referred to it as 'manipulative', 'passive-aggressive' (Dickson, 1982) and 'indirect aggression' (Rees & Graham, 1991). I consider 'indirect communication' to be the most useful term, because the other expressions have a negative judgement attached to them, and imply that indirect communication has an underlying aggressive or malicious intent. I do not consider this always to be the case and in many instances at work an indirect approach can be more easily understood and appreciated by colleagues than an assertive, aggressive or passive one. Indirect communication can be irritating, particularly when it involves using the other person's feelings to encourage them to do something (notably feelings of guilt), or it can be diplomatic and subtle, avoiding the embarrassment on both sides that may come with assertiveness. The following scenario illustrates the various styles of communication outlined above.

Communication scenario

Joe and Sandy are working on preparing a new course together. They have each agreed to complete a separate task and have now met to discuss progress. Sandy has completed her task but Joe, whose wife Debbie has just had a new baby, has not made much progress at all. Here are some possible responses:

Sandy: Well, I've completed the course outlines. How have you got on with the proposal?

Joe (aggressive):   Oh, little miss perfect! How do you expect me to do the proposal with all that I have going on?

[Joe is being defensive, undermining Sandy and inviting a row.]

Joe (assertive)·   I appreciate the work you have put in, Sandy, and I must apologize. I haven't made the progress I had hoped to on my part of the task.

[Joe is acknowledging Sandy's contribution, and recognizing that she deserves an apology rather than excuses. He is also giving her the information she needs to understand what the current situation is. They can now potentially revise expectations together regarding completion of the project].

Joe (passive):   That's great. What do we need to do next?

[Although Joe is flattering Sandy to some extent, he is not taking responsibility for his side of the agreement. He is forcing Sandy to take the lead, and to follow up on his task.]

Joe (indirect –   Wow, that's absolutely brilliant. You are
manipulative):   incredible, Sandy. I wish I had your stamina! Of course, you don't have a new baby to look after, so have probably had some sleep in the last few weeks. I haven't had a single second to do anything and actually, between you and me, I think Debbie has post-natal depression. Don't tell anyone, but she has hardly lifted a finger since the baby was born. Not all women are as amazing as you. Anyway, where were we?

[Joe is completely avoiding telling Sandy he hasn't done the work, but is making it very hard for her to hold him responsible. He is using a combination of overt, inappropriate flattery, guilt and secrecy. Sandy may well be feeling confused, not only about where they stand with the project, but also with the muddle of complicated emotions Joe has stirred up in her.]

Joe (indirect – diplomatic):	OK, that's great. Let's go through the course outlines now and book another session next week to go over the proposal.

[Joe is acknowledging Sandy's contribution, but without resorting to flattery. By putting her contribution at the top of the agenda, he is showing respect for her. He is avoiding admitting his own lack of progress, but is also avoiding burdening Sandy with his own problems, or worrying her by informing her he had not done as much work on it as she has. He has presented the suggestion of another time to go over his contribution, and can use the next week to prepare the proposal. He can even use Sandy's course outline to help him with this.]

As can be seen from the communication scenario, the amounts of stress both Joe and Sandy experience as a result of their communication will partly be determined by their interpretations. Joe's various responses to Sandy's very neutral opening will set the scene for how stressful the remainder of the project actually is. The aggressive and indirect (manipulative) reactions might be typical of Joe, indicating he is a difficult person, thereby putting them both under more stress. Alternatively, his reaction may be a reflection of the stress he is under. How Sandy interprets and responds to this will define whether the project is completed amicably or falls apart. The passive and indirect (diplomatic) reactions might also be typical of Joe. Whether the project works out in these situations will depend on Sandy's response to Joe. If she likes to take the lead, either situation may work out fine. If she decides to force Joe into reciprocity, it could become more stressful for them both. Interestingly, Joe's indirect (diplomatic) response may actually allow them both to feel less stressed as a result of their meeting than any of the other responses and, as long as Joe takes responsibility for completing the proposal in the next week, may not cause any undue problems.

Difficult personality styles

There are many different types of difficult person you can encounter at work, and everyone will respond differently to each one of them. Some people are infuriated by those who tell others what to do, whereas other people are equally infuriated by those who always need to be told what to do. In the hustle and bustle of the world of teaching there are four types of personality that people frequently find difficult to get along with: bossy, manipulative, moody and lazy. Please note, these are exaggerations and no one is defined purely by one aspect of his or her personality. Also, there are many other difficult personalities, but these are some of the easiest to spot. Details on dealing with a fuller range of difficult personalities can be found in Bernstein (2001). Understanding the different types of behaviour will help you understand how to work with different kinds of people, so these difficult personalities will be discussed in more detail after we have tackled behaviours.

General tips on working with difficult people

- *Be polite*. This can be difficult, particularly if the other person is very rude. However, you maintain your self-respect, role-model appropriate behaviour to the other person and avoid stirring them up further. Sometimes when the boss (or another influential person) has a particularly bad communication style, they model it to their whole department, who then treat each other that way. Hence the toxic workplace!
- *Avoid the temptation to reflect back their difficult style*. People who are argumentative encourage arguments. Arguments do not tend to get you anywhere. Passivity will lead to no progress. Indirect, manipulative communication is confusing and over-complicates matters.
- *Try to understand what the difficult person wants*, then subtly communicate to them whether or not you can provide it to them. It may be work, attention, sympathy or a whole range of other things. Only you can decide whether you can fulfil their unreasonable needs.
- *Don't reward (or even tolerate) bad behaviour*. There can be a temptation to give the difficult person what they want to shut them up or make them go away. Rewarding bad behaviour, however, simply encourages more bad behaviour.

- *Do reward good behaviour*. Occasionally even the most annoy-
ing person does something right. When this happens, give
them whatever it is they want, be it praise, attention, a break
or to be left alone. Do not spoil it by criticizing or asking for
more (unless you know they want more work).

Bossy people: the pitfalls

Bossy people's preferred communication style is aggressive. They
get a sense of power and control from dominating other people.
Everyone is familiar with bossy people, as they are frequently
experienced during childhood (this is not a coincidence, as bossy
people find it most satisfying to boss around smaller or weaker
people). At the positive end of the spectrum bossy people can be
decisive leaders who will go to great lengths to explain how
things should be done, and they can be immensely helpful. At
the negative end they can be patronizing, demeaning, petty
bullies, who make the lives of those around them a misery. The
main pitfall of working with a bossy person is that if you allow
yourself to be dominated by them, you will make them feel
better so they will come back for more. Also, because of their
warped perception of human relationships, they may even think
you enjoy being dominated. Don't let them make that mistake
with you.

Strategies for dealing with bossy people

Don't let your usual charming, helpful way of interacting with
people change because of their bossiness. That means you should
work at your own pace, and to your own standard. Do not allow
yourself to be rushed inappropriately, or to work to an inferior
standard just because someone else is rushing you. If the bossy
person is an equal or subordinate you are most likely either
collaborating or doing them a favour, so make it clear you have
your own way and pace of working. If the bossy person is a
superior, negotiate about quality versus speed, but do not allow
yourself to be bullied into spending your own time on the task.
    If the bossy person is your superior and you are consistently

being expected to work beyond what is reasonable, you have two choices (besides the unacceptable one that you make yourself ill by staying in the situation you are in). Either you can leave, or you can stay where you are and make it work for you, in which case, you need to change the situation.

If you want to change the situation, one of the first things you should do is to get into the habit of documenting each interaction. A diary is a good way of doing this, but a computerized file is handy if it comes to producing documentation later. Not only does this help you feel better by getting things out of your system, but it also helps support your case for change. Try to keep it factual and behavioural (focused on times, dates and what happened rather than your interpretations about your boss's personality, motives and so on). Keep it simple, for example, *'On Tuesday, my boss informed me I would have to give an extra three sessions of teaching with only one day's notice and no time to prepare. Extra time required, four hours' preparation, in the evening. Attempt at negotiation and response.'* This is strong enough stated as fact than a much longer statement documenting your feelings and how you think your boss is a slave driver.

Consider approaching your trade union. If you are not a member of a union and are experiencing the above, you would be wise to join. Unions have been effective in supporting teachers who are being overworked, bullied and otherwise subjected to stress, up to and including winning compensation payments. Details of many teacher's unions are included in Further resources (pages 149–51). They can advise you of your rights and even represent you. It is amazing the effect a union representative can have on a bully.

Another approach is to have a heart-to-heart with your boss's boss. You should only do this if you have already given feedback to your boss and it hasn't worked. Again, the documentation becomes invaluable for keeping a record of the facts.

If this situation applies to you, you should turn immediately to the section on 'Knowing when to go' (page 72) and 'Bullying' (pages 84–8). Think seriously about leaving, and make time to apply for other jobs. Seek support in doing so from people away from work.

Lazy people: the pitfalls

Lazy people's preferred communication style is passive. The worst pitfall of working with a lazy person is that they can ruin your own attitude towards work. After all, if they are getting away with doing so little and getting paid the same as you are, why should you care about working hard?

They can also ruin your attitude towards people who assign you work, as you can end up feeling they are taking advantage of you, when in fact they were under the impression you were there to work.

They can also lumber you with a lot of their work, for which they will later take the credit. Sometimes they will accomplish this by trying to be friends, so you feel obliged to do things for them. Others will intimidate you into doing it. In either case, remember who assigns you work and who does not.

Strategies for dealing with lazy people

Think about quality time. Any time you are at work and are not working is a slice taken out of what you will eventually achieve at work. If you really like the lazy person and want to spend time with them, think and decide how much time and stick to your daily allocation. Make a mental note of the time your interaction with them starts and end the interaction once, say, 15 minutes have passed. This will still cost you over an hour a week. Any more and it will cost you too much.

Be a good role model to the lazy person. You may be tempted to become lazy yourself because it seems more fun. However, success is much more fun than stagnation and rustout, which is where laziness leads. Instead, try to stimulate some interest in your lazy colleague and never feel you have to hide your own enthusiasm for work.

Manipulative people: the pitfalls

Manipulative people's preferred communication style is indirect. Manipulative people are essentially devious people. They can't get what they want by asking for it (usually this is too threatening to their fragile egos) or by working for it themselves (there may be an overlap with the lazy variety described above, or they may simply be or think they are incompetent). So they come up with subtle or not so subtle ways of getting people to do what they want through preying on their victims' human weaknesses, whether it be your own not so nice characteristics (vanity, envy, laziness, lack of confidence or dislike of someone else, for example), or your wish to help the manipulative person in their plight.

The strategies they use are wide and varied, but what they have in common is that they result in the manipulative person being exempt from doing something that they clearly should be doing (such as some obvious part of their job), either by getting someone else to do it, in addition to their own tasks, or by performing so badly that no one ever expects anything from them, and no one, including their superiors, dares to challenge them about it for fear of unpredictable consequences. They may also engage in other, seemingly pointless manipulations, such as consistently arriving late to a meeting so that no one else can start, which can simply serve the purpose of making them feel powerful and important.

Strategies for dealing with manipulative people

Manipulative people are extremely slippery and notoriously difficult to deal with. Part of the problem is that they are so focused on getting out of doing what they should be doing, using whatever means necessary, that they are well ahead of anyone who is reasonably committed and expects the same of others.

One of the simplest strategies to use with a manipulative person is to recognize that they need you in some way (certainly more than you need them), and you have the power to fulfil or not fulfil their needs. Then, as subtly as possible, you can work out what it is they want you to do and negotiate with them for it, making sure they pay a reasonable price. For example, if they want to waste your time so that they can avoid getting on with their work, make sure you have in mind a specific time limit to the time-wasting: no more than, say, 15 minutes. If you need something from them, and you haven't got a word in edgeways after 15 minutes, it is quite reasonable to say, '*I'm sorry* [you aren't sorry, but you are communicating in a language they understand by apologizing], *I wish I could chat, but I really have to rush. I just wanted x from you before I go.*' The manipulative person may claim not to have time right now, in which case get them to agree to a specific time and date when they can, make sure it fits with your schedule (allowing at least one working day for them to have 'forgotten' or not got around to it) and hold them to it. At the allotted time, follow up with them, preferably by email or phone message. Stay bright and cheery, as if there is nothing untoward going on, but be firm with them. The job must be done on time, which is why you agreed that date. Take special care not to get angry with them, because they will exaggerate it out of all proportion. You may even end up being accused of being a bully yourself.

Moody people: the pitfalls

Moody people may or may not have a preferred style of communication in terms of aggression, assertiveness and so on, or they may simply be negative in their general demeanour. Moody people may be sullen or grumpy all the time or may have mood swings according to the level of stress they are under, which, as you know, will fluctuate on a day-to-day basis in teaching. Although moody people may seem relatively harmless compared to bossy, manipulative and lazy people, they, too, can be a source of stress. As with all difficult people mixing with them regularly incurs the risk of becoming moody yourself, which will undermine the quality of your working life and, sometimes, your home life too. Moody people also have a way of stimulating feelings of guilt in others like nothing else can – there is always that niggling feeling that if you were a better, kinder person, they would not feel so bad. Do not be fooled.

Strategies for dealing with moody people

Whatever the cause of the person's bad moods you must not take responsibility for it, although there is no problem with creating a pleasant environment for everyone you come into contact with at work. That includes taking care not to be cold or heartless (after all, the moody person is clearly unhappy), while making sure your own mood is not dragged down. So by all means ask how the moody person is, but don't become their counsellor or parent. Sympathetically listen to the first sentence or two of their response and unless they are going through an unexpected tragedy, such as the loss of a family member or a serious illness (in which case, they should be talking to their boss, or personnel, not you), then acknowledge their feelings while closing the conversation down.

Are you a difficult person?

In reading over the material on different behaviours and personalities, you may recognize yourself in the descriptions. Don't worry, because awareness is the first stage in making a change and even becoming more aware of your own patterns will automatically put you in a position to be a little more adaptable with others.

You will no doubt be well aware of why you feel the need to be bossy, manipulative or whatever, and it may be that when you are under stress that is the only way you know how to respond. Responding in other ways may make you feel vulnerable, may not seem effective or may not be what you consider the most appropriate way to behave at work. The trick is recognizing that if other people find you difficult, it will make your life difficult too. So it may be time to try something different.

A good start would be to look at the section on assertive communication in this chapter. You would probably find it helpful to do some further reading on assertiveness (you can look up the references in pages 156–69). It would also help to practise listening skills, focusing not on what you want, but on what the other person is saying. Do they want something from you? Are they giving your feedback? Remember, listening to the spoken part of the message might be more helpful than making assumptions based on their tone, body language, implied motivations and so on. You may also find it helpful to talk to a supportive counsellor, or coach, through the Teacher Support Line. Details are in Further resources (page 150).

Finally it is worth mentioning that a small minority of people may, in fact, have a more serious problem, which would benefit from professional help. If you are suffering from severe or ongoing sleep problems, panic attacks, extreme anxiety, deep or long-term feelings of depression or other emotional difficulties, consider visiting your doctor. These experiences can, in some cases, be symptoms of serious psychological or physical illnesses, many of which can be greatly alleviated by treatment.

Working on yourself

There are many ways of working on yourself, including counselling or psychotherapy, coaching, self-help groups and self-help books. You can find more information on each of these approaches in Chapter 8. However in many cases there is no need to resort to professional help and it can sometimes be detrimental, by making you feel more ill or deficient than you really are. Everyone has strengths and weaknesses and different ways of coping with stress, and there are many ways of working on yourself, simply by becoming more aware of yourself and of other people.

7

BALANCING PROFESSIONAL AND PERSONAL LIFE

Why you should value your home life

Have you ever heard the cliché of someone working so hard that they do not 'know' their own family? Well, like a lot of clichés, it is grounded in reality. While it is great to have a satisfying career, your professional identity is only part of who you are, and it is important to have a life and relationships outside work. You never know if your job will disappear tomorrow, whether through redundancy, illness or any other unknown factor, and if the worst happened you would still need to have a sense of belonging and purpose.

This can be all the more difficult when family and other personal relationships have been neglected. When I worked in rehabilitation, I saw the same situation come up time and time again – strong, capable, competent men and women, whose lives had suddenly and unexpectedly changed through a car accident or an illness, and found their family were like strangers. In some unfortunate cases, having lost their job, people found soon after they also lost their spouse and family. Unknown to them, for a long time it had been their financial support that had kept the family together and without that there was no relationship left. In a few cases, partners, parents and children would become closer and get to know each other for the first time, but sadly this was the minority of cases. Generally, the people whose families thrived in times of adversity were those who had valued their families when things were running smoothly.

How personal relationships are different from professional relationships

In Chapter 6 we looked at difficulties in relationships with people at work, and in particular bossy, manipulative, moody and lazy people. You are equally likely to experience these difficult characteristics in personal relationships, but personal relationships are different from professional relationships in several important ways. Most notably you do not have the clearly defined roles of professional relationships, and you do not have a set of expected behaviours as set out in your job description. Furthermore, normally people engage in personal relationships in order to enhance their emotional well-being, rather than their financial well-being. Therefore, it is up to you to define what your role will be in personal relationships, and you are 50 per cent responsible for ensuring that these relationships are emotionally satisfying. While it is possible to learn to have satisfying relationships both personally and professionally, personal relationships are much less clearly defined and open to negotiation, and learning to enjoy your personal relationships is much more intuitive and less rational than that of professional relationships.

Boundaries in personal relationships

Boundaries are physical or psychological barriers, which protect you. Boundaries that provide a physical barrier offering protection include doors, walls and ceilings. Each of these boundaries protects you – in the case of a door from interference from others within the same building, and in the case of walls and ceilings from noise or from the external elements. Psychological boundaries are similar to physical boundaries but they cannot be seen. You decide upon and define your own psychological boundaries (although many are culturally prescribed), and include such things as choosing to come to work on time, focusing on particular tasks or students and deciding when you have provided enough help to another person.

Boundaries are important in personal relationships, to protect the well-being of both people involved. In relationships, you share many things with other people: space, conversation, each other's attention and physical presence. Sometimes, in the case of like-minded individuals or family members, you share an understanding of how much is enough and how much is too much, although conflicts often arise when the two people in the relationship have different boundaries and expectations of one another. When you are setting boundaries, essentially what you are doing is deciding when you have reached a limit, then making it clear to the other person that limit has been reached.

With work relationships this is actually relatively easy to achieve compared to personal relationships, because it is acceptable to behave relatively unemotionally at work and the expectations of your role are fairly clear. There are even some boundaries that are decided for you – for example, classes start and end at a particular time, certain material is addressed within lessons and students defer to the teachers' knowledge. In personal relationships this is not so straightforward. Friends and family may stretch your boundaries by requesting, demanding or simply taking up too much of your time, space or attention. Setting boundaries in these situations is not simply a matter of assertiveness, it is a matter of deciding and communicating the limits of what you personally can give. Everyone has limits, but some people have greater difficulty understanding when limits have been reached, and setting boundaries when this has happened.

Conflicts between the responsibilities of work and family interfere with both, making work and family life stressful (Frone et al., 1991; Adams et al., 1996). Frame and Hartog (2003) identify teachers as being particularly prone to imbalances between work and other areas of life. They argue that, despite having more autonomy in their working lives, teachers end up working longer hours because of cultural expectations that they will complete their work in whatever hours it takes to get the job done. However, research shows that failure to achieve a good balance between work life and home life can lead to a variety of serious negative consequences for both individuals and organizations, including higher stress levels, increased absenteeism and lower productivity (Hobson et al., 2001). This has finally been recognized in teachers and the *National Agreement* specifies all teachers' right to a work–life balance. Therefore, it is in the interests of your school, as well as yourself, to achieve a good balance between the time you spend working, preparing to work, recovering from work, thinking about work, and the time you spend on other things.

Family relationships

Researchers have now started to recognize that work stress does not only affect people while they are at work, and that the stress they are under is not all caused by work itself. Stress that is generated outside work, for example in the home, will carry over into the workplace, whether you are aware of it or not. In the same way, stress at work will often 'spill over' into your home life and family relationships. If you have both a job and a family you are already fulfilling more than one role (for example: teacher, partner, parent) and many people fulfil several (Kinman & Jones, 2001).

You did not come into the world with predefined roles and as you acquire new roles you must make choices, take on responsibilities and learn new skills. All of these changes are stressful, and these stresses occur simultaneously with any work stress affecting you.

Even when your family is stable it can be a source of stress and worry, as well as a drain on your emotional and physical resources. Dealing with change, and with the unknown, is inevitably more stressful, although it can make life more exciting. Some of the most stressful changes that can occur in your personal life are addressed in this chapter. As you have seen in previous chapters, stress is not always negative, and some of the happiest times are also the most stressful.

New relationships

New relationships can be wonderful at any stage of life, but when you do not yet know the other person well they can also bring up concerns about whether the new person is everything you hope. On the one hand, new people tend to portray themselves in the best possible light, and you have no negative experiences with them to mar the illusion. You are also likely to be presenting yourself in the best possible light. On the other hand, being human, everyone's idiosyncrasies will appear sooner or later. For many people, past relationships have undermined their ability to trust – having trusted someone before and been hurt or even having been responsible for hurting another person, you can doubt that relationships will ever work out for you and try to protect yourself by not getting too involved in the first place. One way of achieving this is by becoming so involved in work that there is no time for other relationships outside the workplace.

The problem with this is obvious – a lonely future and missing out on the possibility of the kind of happiness that only an intimate relationship can provide. While some people genuinely enjoy their own company to the exclusion of others, many more people are isolated and lonely, and simply fear taking the risk of getting involved. If this is the case for you it would be worth you reading Chapter 8, which addresses feelings that may be at the root of your loneliness.

Marriage

Suppose you meet the partner of your dreams, and decide to get married? Can you expect to live happily ever after? Sadly, marriage is consistently rated as one of the most stressful life events you can go through and, according to the most widely used scale of life events, rated as the seventh most stressful life event above being fired, retirement or death of a close friend (Holmes & Rahe, 1967). Many people are disappointed to discover how difficult and stressful getting married can be. It is important to be prepared for this stress beforehand and to make allowances for yourself, such as taking time off to prepare and to relax afterwards. Marriage also takes some adjustment, even if the two people have lived together beforehand, so you should plan your wedding so that you will be able to spend adequate time with one another adjusting to your new relationship.

Once married, you should continue to maintain interests separately as well as together, and take an interest in each other's work and goals. Only by mutual agreement and support can both partners in a marriage develop to reach their full potential. However, sometimes goals can change and a successful marriage allows both partners to change and adapt.

Pregnancy, childbirth and childcare

Pregnancy, childbirth and childcare affect both men and women, and in the current work climate both men and women are expected to cope with the stress resulting from these life-changing events with the minimum of disruption to working life. The supportiveness of employers and co-workers, both practical and emotional, varies greatly from place to place. Yet the added financial burden of children makes it all the more important that you effectively manage the stress resulting from pregnancy, childbirth and childcare while maintaining your professionalism as a teacher.

Pregnancy and childbirth, along with the months and years immediately following the birth of a child, can also be extremely stressful. This can be both surprising and disappointing, especially to people who believe that a family will automatically bring happiness. It can be a great surprise, for example, to discover how exhausted you feel at the very beginning of pregnancy, and you may not have much energy to do much more than simply holding down the requirements of your teaching role. Therefore, it is important that even early in pregnancy, you reduce your expectations of yourself to the minimum.

Ironically it is early in pregnancy when you least believe this is actually happening and no one else can yet see that you are pregnant that many of the worst symptoms are experienced. These vary from woman to woman, and some women are lucky enough to feel happier and healthier during pregnancy. For others, some of the symptoms commonly experienced are detailed below, along with suggestions for alleviating them. See Stoppard (2004) for details of recommended diet and other issues related to pregnancy.

Coping with stress during pregnancy

- *Alleviate morning sickness and nausea* by eating small, frequent meals and snacks, and drinking plenty of water and non-caffeinated drinks.

- *Cope with fatigue by planning your day* to reduce the amount of going up and down stairs and standing around you have to do – this can be difficult when you are teaching, but try to combine trips up and down stairs together rather doing each individual trip, and sit rather than stand whenever possible.
- *Problems with sleeping can be common,* so go to bed early and try to rest during the day. When you awake at night, try not to worry about how tired you are. Use the time to practise relaxation exercises such as the one in Chapter 2 (also see Widdowson, 2003).
- *Mood swings are also common.* Do not involve yourself in workplace disputes. Let off steam outside work by talking to someone sympathetic but not directly involved. A friend or less involved family member, such as a cousin or aunt, would be a better choice than a parent or partner, who might feel worried or responsible.
- *Recognize the impact on your partner.* Smith (2004) is an excellent book for partners during pregnancy.
- *Find out your rights and responsibilities.* The law changes frequently, so ensure the information you have is up to date, particularly regarding the submission of paperwork to your employer. This could make a difference to the maternity pay you are entitled to.

Childbirth is a very personal matter and you should consult your doctor well in advance to plan the birth of your baby. While some mothers choose to work right up until the birth you should not feel under any pressure to do so, and should prioritize your health and the health of your baby. Be aware that, although you will very likely become extremely involved in thoughts about the arrival of your baby, your work colleagues may not feel the same way. Pregnancy and birth can bring up complicated feelings of envy, disinterest or squeamishness in others, and it is unlikely that anyone other than people very close to you will wish to hear the details of your experiences. Keep your comments vague and reasonably upbeat.

While you will very likely find if difficult to cope with balancing parenting and work, your colleagues may be less than sympathetic, particularly if they feel they have to cover for you if you are frequently absent. Remember, too, that some of your colleagues may have had their own difficulties around having children and your new role as a parent may be a painful reminder. Practise the communication techniques described in Chapter 5 and Chapter 6 and be clear that if staff are being expected to do more than is reasonable the responsibility for making up for the shortfall lies with the school, not with individual members of staff. The *National Agreement* specifies that teachers being asked to cover for each other's absences should be a rare occurrence, and should not exceed 38 hours per year. It is not your responsibility to ensure this is adhered to, but it is useful to know about, and assert your awareness of these rights if you feel others are becoming resentful towards you.

Divorce

Divorce is the second most stressful life event after the death of a spouse (Holmes & Rahe, 1967). According to the Office of National Statistics (2004), divorce is still on the increase in Britain. Recent marriage rates have been about 270,000 per year, while divorce rates are nearly 170,000 per year. More often women are granted divorces than are men. The most common reasons for divorce are unreasonable behaviour of men being divorced by their wives, and separation for two years with consent, when men divorce their wives. The age at which people divorce is most commonly their early 40s. Around 150,000 children are affected by divorce each year, a quarter of whom are aged under five. One in five children in Britain are now brought up by one parent (usually by their mothers), while only 2 per cent of dependent children are brought up by lone fathers. About half of lone mothers and a third of their children no longer see the father, but the remainder have fathers who tend to live nearby, with less than a fifth living in another part of Britain or abroad.

Divorce is typically extremely stressful for all concerned and, unlike the stress of getting married, the stress typically goes on for an extended period of time, often years, as roles are renegotiated and relationships are damaged. Divorce is also financially costly, often with legal fees running into thousands of pounds. What this amounts to is people of working age struggling with emotional and financial difficulties, and trying to hold down a job at the same time.

If you are considering divorce, are in the process or have recently divorced, you may benefit from support specifically focused on this process. Relate provide relationship counselling throughout the UK, and more information can be found on their website www.relate.org.uk. Divorce Aid provides information and support on many aspects of divorce, which can be accessed through their website www.divorceaid.co.uk.

Bereavement

Death of a spouse is the most stressful life event (Holmes & Rahe, 1967). More commonly people working in teaching face the stress of losing a parent or friend, and less commonly but more devastatingly, the death of a child. This stress may be worsened by an extended illness prior to death, or by a sudden accident. In any event, it is important to give yourself time to adjust to the loss, and many people benefit from bereavement counselling. Cruse Bereavement Care provides counselling, support and information on bereavement, including telephone helplines. More information is available from their website at www.crusebereavementcare.org.uk.

Coping with family problems

Sadly, rather than being a place of refuge, some families are a source of great stress and even verbal or physical abuse. Readers who are aware of physical abuse occurring within the family are urged to contact their local social services, and/or the police. You can also call the National Domestic Violence Helpline on 0808 2000 247 and speak to a woman, or if you are a man experiencing domestic violence and would prefer to talk to another man, call the MALE helpline (Men's Advice Line and Enquiries) on 0845 064 6800. Verbal abuse is more difficult to identify, because so often it is not the actual words but the way that they are delivered that causes pain. Elgin (1990) provides practical strategies for dealing with verbal attacks, and Brinkman and Kirschner (2002) offer approaches specifically designed for overcoming problems with family members.

Even when things are going well, there is always a certain amount of stress that goes along with family life. However, it is not uncommon for families to experience all manner of problems. These may be to do with the mental or physical health of a family member, academic or occupational difficulties, or inadequate ways of coping with stress. The teenage years may be particularly difficult for all members of a family, particularly if the young person has not learned healthy or adequate ways of dealing with their feelings, or with stress. This can lead to a variety of further stressors, either related to the young person's mood or to their behaviour. Many parents fear their child taking drugs, for example, yet fail to provide the child with alternative ways of socializing or dealing with stress. Such problems can be a great source of shame for the parents, who continue to need to go to work to support the family. Parent Talk provide information, coaching and support to parents, and more information can be found on their website www.parenttalk.org.uk.

Friendships

Friendships can be a great source of support and the joy that is shared between friends can provide you with comfort during difficult times. It can be difficult to predict which friendships are simply relationships of convenience. Enjoyable though they may be, these will not provide support when it is needed. However, it is only by taking the risk and sharing your feelings with others that a friendship has the opportunity to develop. As with intimate relationships, often people fear the betrayal or abandonment of a potential friend, and miss out on developing close friendships as a result.

Community

It is easy to fall into the trap of modern life, of thinking that you operate as an individual, perhaps with significant relationships, but ones that revolve around yourself and your own needs. Less stressful cultures have a more collective approach, which seems to have a protective effect. Recognizing you are part of a larger community can help you to achieve this, and can help you develop friendships and other relationships as a spin-off. Furthermore, social isolation has been found to cause stress on a physical as well as a psychological level, whereas community and social support actually reduces stress (Sapolsky, 2004).

Exactly how you define community will depend on how wide your circle is – it may be a small village or town, or you may feel connected to people in many parts of the world. What is important is finding some way of participating in your community. This does not just have to be about giving, as is often the case in community activities that amount to voluntary work. Following up on your interests by becoming part of a group of others with similar interests can lead to activities that are fulfilling in a way that work and home life is not – by uniting you with a community of like-minded individuals who share your dreams and passions.

You could choose to follow up on a sport or other healthy activity you have always wanted to try or you could choose something really unhealthy, such as wine tasting (if you have heard that wine drinking is beneficial, please note this is only the case for very small, infrequent quantities – for more details see the Department of Health's website at www.dh.gov.uk). You might enjoy reading and could get involved in a book-reading group, or you could develop your confidence and teaching skills (Street, 2007) by taking up amateur dramatics.

8

Managing Feelings

Understanding emotion

Emotions are all about survival. When you were born you had no rationality but you were fully in touch with your emotions. You shouted when you felt angry, hid away when you felt scared, cried when you were hurt or felt sad, lonely or in pain, and these expressions of feeling brought everything you needed to recover quickly from emotional events. This was normal and healthy. During childhood and adolescence you developed rationality and knowledge, and at the same time learned to suppress emotions that were not appropriate to social situations. You found other ways of meeting your needs, based on experience, and learned to fend for yourself rather than cry out for what you wanted. This course of events has had the unfortunate effect of making many adults think that emotions are immature, unnatural, abnormal or unhealthy. Worst of all, some people think that there is no place for emotion in professional work.

The view that emotions are an important part of working life, and that the recognition and understanding of emotions at work are an important step, is beginning to be recognized in research such at that published by authors Ashforth and Humphrey (1995). They argue that emotions are inevitable, even in the workplace. Rather than suppressing your emotions, recognition and understanding of emotional life at work is an important part of effective stress management. In support of this view, research by Mearns and Cain (2003) showed that having the belief that you can control your negative moods reduces stress, burnout and distress in teachers, independent of actual stress level and ability to cope.

Emotions are about survival, even in adulthood. You feel the same discomfort when you are hungry, but you can delay your need for food without expressing unhappiness. Nevertheless, the discomfort felt is what prompts you to eat. That is why people with eating disorders stop eating or overeat – they have trained their brains to interpret the discomfort of hunger or fullness positively rather than negatively. In the same way, when you are in a stressful environment it is perfectly natural to feel angry, sad or fearful, but there is no outlet for those feelings, and suppressing the feelings and their expression simply leads to an acceptance of the unacceptable (and poor health and other problems as described in Chapter 1). Therefore, it is important that you learn to recognize and appreciate your emotions for the protective capacities they have, and give yourself time and space to explore and understand your own feelings. The intention is not to make your emotions go away, but to learn to use your emotions to create the life that is right for you.

When you feel angry

Anger is probably the most socially unacceptable and most misunderstood of all emotions. Anger can make you feel out of control, destructive and inconsiderate towards others, yet anger is a perfectly natural emotion that arises from feelings of injustice.

Many people have had early experiences of being intimidated by someone who was angry, and fear that angry people may become violent. After all, anger is related to the 'fight' part of the 'fight or flight' response that occurs in the body, as described in Chapter 1. However, it is rarely the case that you or anyone else will become violent at work in a school context, despite the wide publicity of these isolated incidents. Anger can be a great source of energy and motivation for positive change rather than a source of destruction when it is recognized and channelled correctly. Anger was the driving force behind the suffragettes, Martin Luther King, Greenpeace and every other activist who has made the world a fairer, more compassionate place.

As stated above, anger typically occurs when some kind of injustice is perceived, whether it is injustice towards yourself or towards others. In teaching, you may feel angry about how you are treated, at how your co-workers are treated or at how your students are treated. Recognize that your moment of anger is a time of insight, when you become aware of the problem of injustice and, often, of the cause of the injustice. The moment of anger will also bring with it immense energy, derived from a huge release of adrenalin, which can be directed towards some kind of solution to that problem. This does not mean losing your temper but rather, using the extra energy available to you to ask questions, finding flaws in the system and suggesting solutions. This level of control can be achieved though combining mental focus and relaxation (such as the exercise in Chapter 2).

You will find that others respect this approach to channelling your anger far more than they do to your brooding away in the corner or snapping at people who do not have the power or the understanding to change things. Furthermore, people are more likely to take notice of what you say when you are angry, as recent research shows that the brain cannot ignore angry voices the way it can with neutral voices (Grandjean et al., 2005).

Sometimes the injustice you perceive is not related to the system, but is simply the frustration of working with imperfect people in an imperfect environment. For this emotion to be useful to you, which it can be, you need to recognize that the problem may lie within yourself if the unrealistically high expectations you have will lead to disappointment again and again. Releasing anger is central to successfully overcoming these feelings (Rubin, 1997). It can be hugely beneficial in these circumstances to work off your anger in some kind of physical way, such as a vigorous session at the gym or a good brisk walk. As you use up the excess adrenalin in your system, be aware of your body working off and *letting go* of the anger. If you hang on to it, it will only keep you awake later, and you will feel tired and grumpy the following day.

If you have excessive amounts of anger to work off on a regular basis, you might find it helpful to engage in some kind of socially acceptable behaviour that lets you release your anger through your voice. It is natural to want to shout when you are angry, and some sports will allow you to do this. Involving yourself in music, especially the louder varieties (particularly if you sing), can also release a great deal of anger and make you feel much better – as long as you allow yourself to *let go* rather than hang on to the anger. So, surprising though it may seem, joining a choir can be a great strategy for anger management!

When you feel scared

Fear is the flip side to anger, as the 'flight' part of the body's 'fight or flight' response. Fear is a natural way for us to protect ourselves from harm by running away from the situation. There are basically two kinds of fear: adaptive fear, which protects you from danger, and less adaptive fear, commonly referred to as 'anxiety', which occurs when the situation is not actually dangerous and there is nowhere for you to run away to, as is the case when you are at work.

The source of teachers' fears tends to be possibilities rather than realities: worrying about not being good enough, not coming across as knowledgeable enough, being humiliated by students and so on. In learning to use fear to your advantage, it is important to distinguish between the two types. If you feel threatened physically by a student, for example, trust your instincts and protect yourself. On the other hand, and much more commonly, if you feel intimidated by the idea of teaching a large group be aware that nerves are a normal part of giving any kind of performance and that teaching is a type of performance. In fact, recent research shows that the use of the elements of acting when teaching, such as animated voice and body, space, humour, suspense and surprise, props and role play, promotes student interest, attention and positive attitudes towards learning, as well as helping the teacher cope with nervousness (Street, 2007).

Jeffers (1987) described her own fear of teaching (as well as other situations) in *Feel the Fear and Do It Anyway*. Her approach to overcoming fear, as the title suggests, is not to try to control the fear before doing what you are afraid of, but to embark on the action you fear, which will then reduce your fear of it. She detailed how, in the teaching of her first lesson, she was terrified but with each subsequent lesson the fear was reduced, until she found she was actually looking forward to teaching.

The same approach can be used for any anxiety-provoking situation at work, yet people lack assertiveness because they fear rejection or anger from the other person. I strongly recommend practising relaxation exercises, such as those described in

Chapter 2, both prior to and, if possible, during, any fear-related situation that does not actually require you to fight or run away!

When you feel sad or hurt

Sadness is often talked about in clinical terms, such as depression. For some reason this seems to be more socially acceptable than simply admitting to feeling low, feeling down, lacking enthusiasm, feeling disappointed, feeling hurt or feeling upset at the loss of someone. Yet these are all normal feelings that mentally healthy people feel at one time or another.

Sadness can be a healthy and natural way of letting go of the past. This may be something as simple as mild disappointment if, for example, you had hoped for sunshine and instead it rained (a situation so common in the UK it hardly seems worth mentioning), or it may be the overwhelming grief that comes with the loss of a friend, partner, parent, sibling or child. In the first case, sadness comes with facing the fact that the day does not fit with your past fantasy of warmth and perhaps a planned outdoor activity. In the second case, sadness come with facing the fact that the person you cared for is no longer there, and perhaps never will be with you again. In both cases, you are faced with reality: you cannot control many of the things in life you would like to. This in turn makes you feel powerless.

By avoiding the natural process of feeling sad, and even crying, you can find yourself stuck in the past, never facing up to the reality of your disappointment or loss but never moving on from it either. This can lead to a complicated process of denial of reality, and difficulty with moving on to the future.

Therefore, in moderation, allowing yourself to feel sad and to express sadness can be very healing. Talking over the disappoint-ment and allowing yourself to cry in the presence of a caring friend or even a trusted professional, such as a doctor or counsellor, can be very beneficial. What is most important in doing this is that you allow yourself to feel and *let go* of what it was you had before, whether real or hoped for. Hanging onto the feelings of sadness, and particularly becoming identified with them, can actually cause more problems. Another kind of problem can develop when you appreciate the comfort you get from the friend or professional so much that you stop wanting to feel better. It can become the whole basis of the relationship, which is not good for either person. Keep in mind how long and how deeply you experience the feelings of sadness. Too much or too long might mean you actually are depressed, in which case you should consult your doctor. The exact amount of time it takes to recover from emotional pain varies from person to person, but if you are still feeling upset by hurt feelings after three months and still feeling grief-stricken six months after losing someone, you should certainly seek help. Saneline (listed in Further resources, page 152) can help you to locate help in your area.

There are many effective antidepressants currently available, but all have side effects. Generally, they will not take effect for several weeks after you have started taking them. You should also be aware that, while they may make you feel better, they won't actually change anything about the situation you are depressed about, so you should work on making real changes in your life while experiencing the elevated mood and energy that comes with treatment.

It is also worth knowing that a number of studies have shown that regular aerobic exercise three times per week for 20 minutes or more is equivalent in effect to antidepressants currently available. For example, Babyak et al. (2000) compared depressed people taking a commonly prescribed antidepressant with people taking a four-month course of aerobic exercise, and a third group taking both the antidepressants and the exercise. Not only did the exercise group get just as much positive effect as those on medication, they were significantly less likely to relapse ten months afterwards. Not bad when you consider that it will also be doing you good rather than putting toxins into your system. You should, of course, consult your doctor before starting any exercise routine.

When you need help coping with your feelings

There are times in life when, for whatever reason, you need help coping with your feelings. There is nothing wrong with that and often such help can come from a supportive friend or relative. Occasionally, however, you do not have this option available to you, or maybe you do not want to discuss your feelings with family or friends in the kind of depth you feel you need. There is a range of options available for such times including counselling or psychotherapy, self-help groups, telephone helplines and self-help books. I will briefly outline the techniques described above, and also make some suggestions for how you can work on overcoming your feelings alone.

Counselling and psychotherapy

Counselling or psychotherapy is a process that involves meeting with a trained professional to work through your problems. Counsellors and psychotherapists vary a great deal, in terms of training, theoretical approach, personality, beliefs and so on, and it is most important that you feel comfortable with the counsellor as a person, rather than simply judging their ability to help you on how much training they have had, or their success with other people.

Counselling normally involves meeting privately at the counsellor's office and talking through your difficulties, often for about 50 minutes, once per week for a number of weeks. Traditional psychotherapy typically goes on for several years, but these days many counsellors use brief therapy techniques, focused on finding solutions to short-term problems. There are advantages and disadvantages to both types of counselling. Traditional psychotherapy will give you plenty of time to get to the root of your problems, often through discussing childhood experiences. This will help you understand how you came to relate to people the way that you do. However, it may be a long time before you feel any benefit from this process, and many people find it frustrating.

Brief therapy produces quicker results but people sometimes

find their problems coming up again and again, often in different guises, because they don't really get to the root of their problems. Whichever approach you use be sure to find out the financial cost, which varies greatly, and how long you are expected to attend counselling before you feel better. If you are considering counselling it is worth talking to your GP, as there are many counsellors working in doctor's practices and this could save you a lot of money. Also, find out if counselling services are available to staff at your school. It is not common for counsellors to be based in schools in the UK, although it is common in North America, and they can sometimes offer supportive services or consultation to teachers as well as students.

If you are considering starting counselling or psychotherapy, visit the websites of the British Association for Counselling and Psychotherapy (BACP) at www.bacp.co.uk, and the British Psychological Society (BPS) at www.bps.org.uk. Both sites will give you credible information from the regulatory bodies of these professions, and you can check whether any counsellor, psychotherapist or psychologist is registered with them. These organizations are there to protect the public and regulate the professions (ensure people are qualified), and it costs you nothing to use them.

Coaching and mentoring

Coaching is a supportive approach that has been used for many years in sports, and has become more prominent in recent years in the professional realm. Coaching differs from counselling in that it focuses on improving the overall performance of the individual, rather than seeking solutions to their problems. The assumption of coaching is that the individual is competent, in control of their life and not 'damaged', and the coach offers feedback to help the individual achieve their goals and perform even better. It is more like teaching than counselling, although the process of learning comes from facilitating the individual to come to their own conclusions, rather than being a passive recipient of knowledge. Coaching can be provided on a one-to-one basis, in a similar way to counselling, or it can be conducted in a group setting. There is normally a fee for coaching, although online coaching is provided without charge through the Teacher Support Network (see Further resources, page 150, under Teacher Support Line).

Mentoring is a less formal approach than coaching, but can be longer term. A mentor is a more experienced, usually older, member of the profession, who fulfils a supportive role in encouraging, guiding and teaching the mentee (or protégé), with the goal of assisting them to become more effective and accomplished professionally. Mentoring is undertaken, usually voluntarily, by a senior professional who wishes to contribute to the learning of a less experienced person in the same profession. There is not normally a charge for mentoring, although it may be part of someone's professional role to mentor newer members of staff, and there may a reciprocal arrangement whereby the protégé gives some professional assistance to the mentor, such as updating the mentor on recent advances in the field.

The process of mentoring dates back thousands of years, at least to the fifth century BC with Socrates and Plato, and mentoring has always been closely allied with teaching, training and professional development. The process of formal mentoring is becoming more acceptable in some professions than super-vision, which implies a disciplinary role. Although mentoring is not an equal relationship, it is a very positive relationship and there is an assumption that the protégé is being groomed to achieve eventually what the mentor has, so it is a very respectful process on both sides.

If you are interested in having a mentor, you could approach a more senior and experienced teacher informally and ask if they would be interested in mentoring you. Normally, someone would be flattered to be asked to be a mentor as it implies admiration and the wish to emulate. How you conduct the mentoring relationship is for the two of you to work out (unless it is organized formally, in which the amount of contact time required may be specified). You could, for example, meet for lunch once a month to talk about how things are going. Some mentors prefer that their protégés contact them only when they have a problem. I have had several mentors for different roles over the years and have found the relationship to be most effective when there is a combination of simply meeting and talking about work and our experiences, and the mentor being available when problems arise, to talk them through.

Group therapy and self-help groups

Group therapy has a similar goal to counselling, except that instead of meeting with the counsellor individually, several clients with similar difficulties meet together with a therapist for a group discussion. Sometimes group therapy involves 'psycho-education', in which the therapist presents information to help the clients learn about their condition or difficulty, although it would normally involve some facilitated discussion or exercises afterwards. Groups are quite small, usually consisting of fewer than ten participants. As is the case with counselling, there may or may not be a fee.

Group therapy is usually 'closed', meaning the group of people participating commit to the whole course of treatment and new people do not join the group. It is usually for a set number of sessions. However, sometimes groups are intended to give ongoing support, in which case they may be 'open', meaning people can choose to leave the group or join the group when there is space. There may even be 'drop in', meaning that the participants know the time and place and can turn up whenever they wish, without having to book themselves in or make a commitment to a certain number of sessions. As there is a counsellor running the group, they run less risk of becoming undisciplined than self-help groups, described below.

Self-help groups are similar to group therapy in that you meet, often on a weekly basis, to discuss your problems. The difference is that you meet and talk with other people who have the same kind of problem, to discover solutions and ways of coping without the assistance of a counsellor. Many people prefer self-help groups because they feel they get a better level of understanding from others who are going through the same kinds of problems. People often feel it overcomes the power imbalance between counsellor and client that may be problematic in counselling. On the other hand, people can become dependent on self-help groups (although they can also become dependent on counselling), and sometimes people feel they don't want to get better because if they did they would lose the support of the group. Furthermore, some self-help groups can be undisciplined, and can be 'taken over' by charismatic or controlling members of the group. However, self-help groups are a relatively inexpensive way of gaining support from others, which can be particularly helpful if you have a lot to talk about but do not want to burden co-workers, family or friends.

The most famous self-help group is Alcoholics Anonymous (AA), which is open to everyone and has meetings every day, throughout the day and evening, all over the world. There is great variation between groups and anyone considering using AA is encouraged to try different groups to find one that 'fits' (details are in Further resources, page 152). AA has a philosophy and a 12-step process that participants are encouraged to work through at their own pace. A process of 'sponsorship', which is similar to mentoring (see pages 124–5) is also used, and can be great source of support. Since the success of AA many more 12-step groups have been set up along similar lines, often with the word 'Anonymous' in the title. Your local newspaper is a good source of information on which groups are active in your area.

Helplines

Telephone helplines are an increasingly popular way of getting support. They offer the opportunity to discuss your problems with a sympathetic person, who is normally trained in counselling skills and knowledgeable about the problem (although not often a fully qualified counsellor). As with self-help groups, helplines are normally focused on specific problems, and can give very detailed help and advice on certain kinds of difficulties. Helplines also have the advantage that they are available whenever you need them, often 24 hours per day, and the cost is only the price of a telephone call (some are even free). Again, this is a good way of getting problems off your chest without having to burden others in your life. Another advantage is that you can remain anonymous. However, helplines are not typically a long-term solution.

Self-help books

Self-help books are an excellent way of working on your problems and improving your life in complete privacy, at your own pace and all for the cost of a book (or less, if you use the library). There are so many self-help books on the market that many bookshops have a whole section, or at least a shelf, devoted to them. They are also very targeted to the problem you are having, so if you feel angry you can get a book on anger management, whereas if you are grouchy because you are overweight you can get a book on weight loss. They range from very basic to very advanced, depending on how deeply you want to understand and address the problem. They are normally written by people who understand the problem well, and who are often experts in the field. Therefore, the information in many self-help books is more accurate and up to date than that you would get from a counsellor.

The key to making self-help books work for you is actually to use them! Your efforts need to begin, not end, with buying the book, and if you really want to help yourself you should set aside time each week to read and work through the exercises with the same level of commitment you would have if you were attending counselling. This takes considerable self-discipline and some-times planning ahead. If you follow the advice carefully, you should see improvements.

Self-help books are also useful even if you don't think you have a problem. They can raise your awareness of issues you didn't know were affecting you, and therefore make you more effective at work and in other social situations. Many of the books I have recommended throughout are useful to anyone interested in managing stress and dealing with people effectively, not just people with problems.

9

Managing Your Health

You may feel tempted to skip this chapter if you do not have a diagnosis of a health problem. However, it is important to recognize that wellness and illness exist on a continuum, which means that you are not either ill or well but simply relatively ill or relatively well. Your position on the continuum will change on a day-to-day basis and if your stress level rises beyond your ability to manage that stress successfully, it is likely to manifest in one or more physical symptoms. Having the goal of optimal wellness will help you manage stress much more effectively than aiming simply for the absence of illness. Therefore I would recommend you at least read the section on taking care of yourself later in this chapter.

Chronic and acute health problems

Put simply, chronic health problems are long-term conditions, whereas acute health problems are short-term conditions. The terms 'chronic' and 'acute' in no way indicate how severe a problem is, but rather how long the person concerned has or is likely to have had the problem. Some conditions are always chronic or acute, but sometimes an acute problem can turn into a chronic one. It is important to recognize that both chronic and acute health problems can impact your stress levels in the short and long term.

Chronic health problems are those that go on for an extended period of time. Often they are problems for which there is no 'cure', although medical assistance may help with controlling the symptoms, and in some cases may prevent the disease from progressing.

Some chronic health problems are widely acknowledged as being serious, for example cancer, HIV (that causes AIDS) and rheumatoid arthritis. If diagnosed with such a condition you would expect to need support from others, disability rights and probably time off work without question. Other chronic health problems are less widely acknowledged as being serious, for example irritable bowel syndrome (IBS), migraine and allergies. Yet this latter group of chronic health problems can lead to long-term discomfort and may even be a greater source of stress for those who experience them, precisely because such conditions are rarely taken seriously. These problems are difficult to deal with, particularly as they may lead to embarrassment and even the implication of malingering if support, rights or time off work are requested. This, in turn, can lead to people who are suffering from less serious chronic conditions denying their own need for support or medical attention and feeling they are exaggerating the problem in their own minds. Unfortunately, if left untreated, not only can such conditions lead to ongoing stress, but also more serious medical problems.

Acute health problems are short-term, and have the potential to be cured or to heal on their own. This does not mean they are not serious – someone involved in a serious car accident will be acutely unwell, and may be in more danger of imminent death than someone with a long-term untreatable condition. When you experience an acute health problem you presume that there will be a period of healing, lasting from days to months, and then you can resume your previous lifestyle. This is not a sensible way forward for two reasons. Firstly, no matter how well you have healed, the illness has taken its toll on your health and you are therefore weaker than you were before the illness or injury. Secondly, acute health problems should be seen as a warning sign that all was not well in your previous lifestyle.

Seeing acute health problems, particularly those arising from accidents, injuries or infections, as merely caused by bad luck is a dangerous response, but all too commonly people in this situation deny any responsibility for what happened, or for preventing it from recurring. Rather than taking more care and learning from the choices they made at the time of the accident, injury or infection, they insist it was not their 'fault' and they 'did nothing wrong'. To consider illness to be a matter of fault is to misunderstand the purpose of reflecting on your own actions – blaming others does not bring about positive change in your life, but keeps you stuck in the past, whereas positive change can come from learning to take better care of yourself.

In some situations, car accidents being a good example, there are not only physical consequences, such as broken bones, wounds and whiplash, but also psychological consequences, such as post-traumatic stress disorder (PTSD). Not everyone who experiences traumatic stress develops PTSD. It is interesting that several studies have found that people who have developed PTSD as a result of a car accident for which they consider themselves to be responsible not only experience milder symptoms initially, but also recover more quickly than people who blame someone else for the accident (Delahanty et al., 1997; Hickling et al., 1999).

Recognize the warning signs

Clearly chronic and acute health problems can both cause stress and be exacerbated by stress. Stress can then become a way of life. Not only is this unhealthy, but it means you miss out on much of the pleasure life has to offer. As stress becomes more and more acceptable to you, you can end up becoming a martyr to work, only to take time off sick when you push yourself too far. If any of this seems familiar to you, it is time to recognize the warning signs, and start to make time for real recovery.

Warning signs

- *Chronic pain persisting beyond the normal period of recovery (typically 6–12 months) following an injury.
- *Headaches, particularly if they occur once a week or more.
- *Feeling tired all of the time.
- *Difficulty sleeping.
- Dealing with tiredness by using stimulants (such as tea, coffee, cigarettes, herbal stimulants) rather than immediate rest.
- Skipping meals or going more than five hours without eating something.
- Putting off visits to the toilet to 'save time'.
- Putting off getting drinks of water when thirsty, for half an hour or more.

[* *Make an appointment to discuss this with your doctor, as it may indicate a more serious problem.*]

If you recognize any of these warning signs, start to make changes to your routine today, and prioritize changing your habits to support your health. Dealing with chronic pain, including headaches and backache, can be difficult but in many cases it is related to poor management of stress. While you should always take headaches and backache seriously as potential symptoms of physical difficulties, and should consult your doctor if they persist, there are several ways you can overcome these problems if they are stress-related.

See your pain as a message from your body that it is being mistreated in some way. Instead of rushing to take painkillers, try to understand that message. Start by looking for the most obvious causes: have you been reading or working in the same position for more than an hour? If so, take a break of at least ten minutes, relax, move around, rotate your neck. Have you been holding your breath, even for short bursts, over the past hour? If so, practise the two-minute relaxation exercise in Chapter 2, and ensure your breathing continues to be regular and deep. Have you eaten in the past three hours? Have you had a drink of water in the past hour? If not, try eating and drinking and see if your pain goes away. Sometimes we have parts of the body where we habitually hold tension, without being aware of it. This can often be the site of an old injury, or a part of the body that holds some anxiety for us (see Chapter 2 for more details). Think about whether you are doing this, and consciously let go of the tension. This can take a lot of practice to achieve, but it is well worth the effort. Finally, think about whether you have had enough sleep. Sometimes aches and pains are simply the result of tiredness.

Health-promoting habits

The following will improve how you feel greatly if practised regularly:

- Practise the relaxation exercise described in Chapter 2 at least once per week.
- Practise conscious relaxation when you have difficulty sleeping.

- If you are chronically tired, there are some simple steps you can take that will improve your sleep in the long term. Go to sleep and get up at the same times each day, expose your eyes to sunlight (without looking directly at the sun) for at least half an hour early in the day and unwind for two hours before bedtime.
- Carry a bottle of water with you and sip throughout the day.
- Visit the toilet at least once per hour. You should also ensure your students get a break to visit the toilet at least once per hour.
- Carry cereal bars with you so that you always have a snack if you do not have time for breakfast or lunch.
- Talk to your doctor about whether vitamin supplements would be suitable for you.

Cigarettes, alcohol and drugs

I hardly need add that substances such as nicotine, alcohol and caffeine only help alleviate stress in the very short term. This short-term respite from stress can make them very attractive as a way of managing stress, and they are widely accepted as such but, as is now well documented, it is a poor solution that leads to many more problems. In the longer term they add to stress on the body and mind, not only by introducing toxins that the body then has to expel, but also by introducing the psychological complication of addiction, leaving you feeling worse without the substance than with it. Obviously, the same goes for any other drugs, whether legal or illegal. Although drinking may seem to help you cope and relax there are many drawbacks, such as argumentativeness with family and friends, physical after-effects and cost (Orford et al., 2002a). Having a drinker in the family presents many difficulties for relatives (Orford et al., 2002b). Incidentally, the use of illegal drugs adds greatly to the stress of the user, as people who use illegal drugs are continually concerned about the consequences of being caught. These consequences can be serious and extremely destructive to your career so frankly, if you are indulging in such activities, you are strongly advised to find a less stressful way of managing your stress! The many alternatives included in this book should be a start.

If you have been using substances to help you cope with stress and feel you would like or need help in stopping, there are many resources that can help you. Quitline can help with giving up smoking and more advice can be found on their website www.quit.org.uk. You can also call them free on 0800 00 22 00. Alcohol Concern have a searchable database on their website so that you can find services in your area to help. Their website is www.alcoholconcern.org.uk. If you want help with a drug-related problem you can talk to an experienced drug worker, free of charge, on the UK National Drugs helpline. Their phone number is 0800 77 66 00. These helplines are confidential. Alcoholics Anonymous (AA) and Narcotics Anonymous (NA) provide self-help groups throughout the world. More details, including local meetings, can be found on their websites at www.alcoholics-anonymous.org.uk for AA and www.ukna.org for NA.

Caffeine, present everywhere in our culture, is a particularly difficult drug to give up. However, it does exacerbate the symptoms of stress and, because its effects are long-lasting, it can disrupt sleep if it is consumed after 2.00pm. I can say from personal experience that giving up caffeine is one of the quickest and most effective ways to become calmer, although if you stop suddenly (cold turkey) expect excruciating headaches for about two weeks afterwards. (For me, the enhanced deep and restful sleep and focused mind made it well worth it.) You can also buy drinks that contain green tea, which contains caffeine but in a milder and more lasting form. This will give you the stimulant effects of caffeine but in a gentler way, rather than the jolt-and-crash you get from coffee or, to a lesser extent, tea. Tea, in particular green tea, has been found to have beneficial effects on long-term health, so drinking tea early in the day may contribute to your long-term wellness. If you hope to manage stress, avoid high-caffeine 'energy' drinks and 'health food' stimulants such as guarana. They will keep you hooked on caffeine, and are potentially dangerous if you develop a stress-related condition.

Enjoying taking care of yourself

Taking care of yourself can sometimes seem like hard work, or a like a luxury you cannot afford. Neither view is correct. With the right attitude, taking good care of yourself with a healthy diet, adequate sleep and waking relaxation, regular exercise and enjoyable forms of recreation, can be an affordable way to a great quality of life. These things are available to you, for little or no cost. What they do require is some foresight and planning, for which you may feel you do not have the mental energy. However, once you free yourself of the mental clutter of worrying about not doing these things, it is amazing how little mental effort is actually required. Getting into routines that support a healthy lifestyle means that these activities require even less mental effort. It becomes enjoyable when you start to feel the benefits of more rest, a clearer mind and the ability to cope with whatever life throws at you.

If you have a chronic disability or illness, think about ways you can improve your quality of life. Make this a priority. Do not fall into the trap of feeling like a victim, or being a martyr to your condition. There are many positive role models of people with chronic illnesses or disabilities who have made great accomplishments, and maintain the best quality of life possible. Decide to have this for yourself.

Some people with chronic illnesses and disabilities fear that, if they enjoy life, people will stop taking care of them. This is incorrect. People who genuinely care about you would be delighted if you could enjoy your life more, so practise assertiveness and let them know what you want and need. Ask for their support in trying new things. What carers and helpers most want is for you to be as happy as you can be, and to be part of making that happen. They also want your appreciation and gratitude, so be sure to give them plenty!

Getting treatment

If reading any part of this book has brought up health concerns for you, the first person you should talk to is your doctor. Your doctor is aware of your medical history and is the best person to advise you on appropriate courses of treatment. Your doctor should also be kept informed of any new complaints and can refer you for tests, or to see a specialist, if appropriate. This relates to both physical and emotional problems. Do not assume that because you have sought treatment in the past that you will not receive adequate treatment now. New treatments are being developed all the time, and a specialist may have access to treatments your GP is unaware of.

You should also discuss with your doctor any alternative treatments you are considering. Doctors vary in their attitude towards complementary therapies, ranging from strong advocates to staunch sceptics. Generally, the least invasive and toxic the treatment, the least stress it will cause you in the long run. Therefore, consider treatments such as physiotherapy before thinking about strong painkillers or surgery. However, it is important to consult your doctor, as there may be reasons they want to advocate some treatments and encourage you to avoid others. A collaborative relationship with your doctor is the best way for you to be informed and involved in your own treatment, both of which are important to your empowerment and sense of control. If you do not see eye to eye with your doctor, consider changing doctors to one that you get along with. Ask around for recommendations, particularly from others who suffer from similar complaints.

Complementary therapies and alternative medicine cover a wide range of different approaches, which range in their credibility and effectiveness. Some, such as acupuncture, have a strong body of research supporting their use, while others are less well supported. Try to find out more about the therapy you are considering before taking the plunge. Most importantly, check the credentials of the therapist. Make sure that they are a member of a professional body, which is there to protect you as a member of the public.

Therapies that are particularly effective in treating stress are biofeedback, acupuncture and massage. Biofeedback is a process whereby your body's physical responses are recorded on a computer and fed back to you in real time, so that you can learn to gain control over your stress responses. Acupuncture is an ancient Chinese method, involving the use of needles to affect the flow of energy around the body (obviously, you should check the acupuncturist uses new needles each time before embarking on treatment). Massage involves the rubbing of muscles to release tension. Reflexology is also very effective, and is a kind of foot massage that uses pressure points in a similar way to acupuncture. These are just a few examples of complementary therapies, which can make a huge difference to how you feel. The biggest advantage of them over mainstream medicine is that they do not involve the use of drugs or further trauma to the body.

Some of these therapies are quite time-consuming, but massage can even be done at school (with your manager's support). Some teachers have been successful in gaining the support of their headteacher in having a masseuse come into the school and massage the teachers' neck and shoulders. In one school, each teacher received ten minutes over two days, during which time the headteacher covered their class. The masseuse was recruited through a massage school and volunteered her time. When she had finished, she commented that the teachers were the tensest people she had served (National Education Association, 2006).

10

STRESS
MANAGEMENT
FOR LIFE

Putting it all together

So, you've made it to the last chapter! Well done.

It is possible that you now feel even more stressed because of all these different things you need to do. You might be thinking, *'It was easier before, when I just had my job to do. Now I need to look after my health, learn to communicate differently, be understanding to horrible people I loved to hate, change my diet, go to bed earlier and stop taking it out on my family! If I wasn't stressed before, I am now!'*

The thing to remember is that change doesn't have to happen all at once. It can happen gradually without you even noticing. You do not need to put yourself under more pressure to benefit from this book. You can work at your own pace, and there are different ways of putting it all together into a successful, stress-managed lifestyle.

One of the most important steps to take in putting it all together is to be realistic and honest with yourself. If you know you are terrible at sticking to diets, don't set yourself up to fail by telling yourself you need to change your diet completely. Instead, choose one thing that you know would either be very easy for you to incorporate, for example taking a multi-vitamin with your breakfast each day, or would give you a substantial reward and make you feel really good about yourself, such as eating one healthy food you have really wanted to try for a while, this weekend. Go ahead – it's good for you!

Once you have taken the first step and realized how easy or pleasurable it is, it will become easier to do it again, and to add to it with other ideas you have thought of while reading this book. Gradually you will incorporate more healthy behaviours and activities into your routine, or treat yourself to the things you enjoy. You will find your quality of life improves gradually, and your stress reduces. The first step is the most difficult but once you have started it will get easier and easier to choose to do the things that make you feel better, not worse.

Projecting a professional image

'*What does a professional image have to do with stress?*' I hear you ask. Well, quite a lot. For one thing, if you appear professional, you are more likely to be treated professionally. For another, consider for a moment that your role at work is like the role in a play or film. It would be so much less believable if the actors were not in costume, but in their own everyday clothes. If you behave convincingly professional, you are professional. Your goal in projecting a professional image is to present yourself in a way that will convince everyone – superiors, peers, support staff, students and the public – that you are indeed a competent, professional teacher. To achieve this goal successfully you should look the part and act the part.

Maybe you think looking professional shouldn't matter. Well, perhaps you are right, but for the majority, professional people looking the part helps put them at ease. Imagine you wanted to talk to a police officer for some reason. How would you feel talking to one in uniform, denoting their role and responsibilities, compared to how you would feel talking to the same person in their everyday clothes? You must admit the uniformed police officer has instant authority compared to the person in jeans and a T-shirt. Many teachers enjoy not having a uniform, but you need to compensate for the lack of automatic authority a uniform provides by projecting your authority in your dress, demeanour and communication style.

This is not to say that everyone should rush out and buy business suits for work – that would probably project a very different image from the one you hope to achieve as a supportive and approachable teacher. You need to be seen as accessible, approachable and as a realistically achievable role model to your students. The clothing you choose affects your students' respect for you as a teacher, as a competent professional and as a representative of the school. Looking as if you rolled out of bed into the first thing you found on the floor does not create a sense of respect for yourself, your students or the school.

Developing an attractive and appropriate professional image can also help you manage stress, as a form of self-nurture. A little indulgence and feeling good about your appearance can make you feel masses better about your life, whether you are male or female, old or young, fat or thin, married or single, gay or straight. If this seems beyond your comprehension that may in itself be a source of stress, for example in helping you relate to others. While image consultancy may cost a fortune, fortunately there are many excellent books on this subject, and a variety of high street clothing shops for every budget and taste.

The entire 'What Not to Wear' series provide exquisite detail of all aspects of modern dress, especially for women. *Dress Your Best* shows how both men and women can effectively dress different body types, and includes sections for work, weekend and evening for all types. I would also recommend *What Your Clothes Say About You* to raise your awareness of how different thoughtless ways of dressing reveal much more psychological information about you than you would expect, although this is primarily focused on women.

Colour, which makes perhaps the biggest difference to your appearance and apparent self-confidence, has been tackled really well by Carole Jackson in her two books, *Color Me Beautiful* (for women) and *Color For Men*. Despite having identified a method of dramatically improving your appearance through correct use of colour, her 'seasons' theory has more recently become unpopular as she correctly discouraged most people from wearing black. Many people want to wear black, and believe that it suits everyone, so the Color Me Beautiful organization abandoned Jackson's approach and unfortunately compromised what it had to offer. However, if you can get your head around it, the seasons theory really works and Jackson's books, although a little dated, do provide timeless advice on dressing correctly for your proportions and selecting classic clothing such as suits. Details of all of these books are available in Further resources, pages 154–5.

Developing a professional image

- *Stay up to date*. This makes you appear in touch with the modern world, and more a part of current events.

- *Dress to suit your body shape and colouring.* This will make you appear more organized, professional and healthy, regardless of the style you choose.
- *Tend towards moderation.* Avoid extreme styles and your classic appearance will last a lifetime. This also overcomes problems such as appearing dated, sexually provocative, frumpy or eccentric.
- *Invest in quality.* This will improve your appearance, save you money and time, and give you more enjoyment.

Summary of previous chapters

In this book, you have seen how teachers experience a range of stressors. In Chapter 1, definitions of stress in the academic literature were presented and you saw how complex the body's responses to perceived stressors are, and how you are affected depends on your interpretation. In reviewing the literature, you saw that teachers were subject to considerable stress at work because of the dynamics of teaching itself, teachers' professional identity and the politics of teaching. The phenomenon of burnout was introduced as a combination of emotional exhaustion, withdrawal from work relationships and a lack of personal accomplishment. You were encouraged to take the practice of stress-management techniques seriously, given the dangers of stress to your physical and mental health, and its detrimental effects on quality of life and career progression.

In Chapter 2, you gained a deeper understanding of stress and your own experience of stress in particular. You discovered that there is a relationship between the stress you experience and how you actually perform, and that there are positive as well as negative aspects of moderate stress. A test enabled you to evaluate your current levels of stress, and action plans were presented that will enable you to take action if you find you are under too much stress.

Chapter 3 gave you insight into stress in teachers specifically. You gained an understanding of three major sources of stress for teachers: the process of teaching itself, your self-image as a teacher and the politics of teaching. You were given tips for dealing with all three types of teacher stress.

In Chapter 4, you explored career development for teachers. You reflected on the various motivations you might have for teaching, and gained an understanding of how your own personal career goals might actually cause you more stress. Added to this, you considered how you could direct your energy towards goal achievement, dealing with self-promotion, and the importance of using feedback rather than feeling defeated by it.

Workplace relationships are always a potential source of stress, and those experienced by teachers are no exception. In Chapter 5, you looked at the importance of reciprocity in relationships and abiding by relationship rules, and then went on to look at tackling the problematic situations of power plays and bullying in the workplace.

Continuing with the theme of interpersonal relationships at work, Chapter 6 focused on dealing with difficult people. You learned to distinguish between people's personalities and their behaviours. In particular you gained an understanding of aggressive, assertive, passive and indirect behaviours, as well as bossy, manipulative, moody and lazy people. You gained further insights into the process of dealing effectively with difficult people at work by looking at the pitfalls of working with each of the difficult personality types, and with strategies for making your interactions with them more effective.

In Chapter 7, you addressed the importance of balancing professional and personal life in effectively managing occupational stress. You came to recognize key differences between personal and professional relationships, and explored the stresses associated with new relationships, marriage, pregnancy, childbirth, childcare, divorce and bereavement. You also obtained advice and ideas of where to seek further help in these circumstances.

Chapter 8 gave you an understanding of emotions such as anger, fear and sadness, including their purpose, and suggestions of how to manage them. You also found out about various ways you can get help with coping with your feelings, including what you can expect from counselling and psychotherapy, self-help groups, telephone helplines and self-help books.

Chapter 9 gave you pointers on managing your health. You discovered the differences between chronic and acute health problems, and how both can affect your stress levels in different ways. You also learned to recognize the warning signs you might experience when stress has started to affect your health. You then gained information about the kinds of habits that will help to promote your health and to counteract the effects of stress. You also gained some basic information on obtaining appropriate treatment, including complementary therapies.

In this final chapter, you are reviewing information provided throughout the book. You have covered the integration of the material covered previously, with some final advice on projecting a professional image. In the remainder of this chapter, you will review the techniques included throughout the book and end with the conclusion.

Summary of techniques

Start by developing an understanding of stress, what it is, and how it can affect you. Identify whether you are under too much stress by taking the stress test in Chapter 2. You can then address your stress with the two action plans that follow. The first action plan is for managing the symptoms of stress in teaching, and is a useful starting point. This consists of developing a positive attitude, practising stress-management skills, identifying sources of support and learning effective communication skills. Stress-management skills included in Chapter 2 are the two-minute relaxation exercise, progressive muscle relaxation (PMR), meditation, self-hypnosis, time-management skills and exercise. The second action plan is for managing the causes of stress in teaching, and is important for longer-term stress management. This consists of identifying whether you have 'burnout' or 'rustout', evaluating your workplace culture, considering discussing stress with your manager and deciding whether it is time to stop or time to go.

Chapter 3 will help you identify specific issues related to stress in teaching. Familiarize yourself with the Education and

Inspection Act, and your school's behaviour policy. Use a humanistic approach to teaching, and respond directly to problems in the classroom. Develop a positive image of teaching and yourself as a teacher, and keep a realistic sense of the control you have in the classroom. Collaborate with colleagues and inspectors to gain recognition for what your school does well, and focus on improving areas that need work.

A self-reflection exercise is included in Chapter 4, exploring what kind of teacher you are. Consider your own personal career goals as a potential source of stress, and focus on directing the energy generated by that stress towards achievement of your goals. Address the need for self-promotion in your future success, and learn to recognize setbacks as a source of feedback rather than failure. Develop a sense of timing in making career decisions.

As a major source of stress at work is relationships, strategies to help you to manage your relationships with both colleagues and students are included in Chapter 5. The basis for effective interactions with others is developing reciprocal relationships with colleagues and with students. It is also important to understand relationship rules and how they apply to your dealings with colleagues and with students. When people break the rules of relationships, you will need to recognize and respond appropriately to power plays from colleagues and from students, and to deal effectively with bullying by colleagues and by students.

The theme of relationships continues with strategies for dealing with difficult people in Chapter 6. These strategies will help you to distinguish between people's personalities and their behaviour, and to understand the various behaviours people engage in at work, which include aggressive, assertive, passive and indirect behaviours. Look at the general tips on working with difficult people to make immediate improvements to your working relationships, and be more selective in your use of the strategies for dealing with bossy, manipulative, moody and lazy people.

With all this focus on work, it is easy to forget that your home life affects your professional life through good times as well as bad. Chapter 7 emphasizes the importance of balancing your professional and personal life. Recognize that to flourish, your personal relationships need your time and attention, and simply bringing home a pay cheque is not enough to ensure a happy marriage or family. Life events such as marriage, divorce and having children can be a considerable source of stress, particularly when you are expected to continue to function at work. Use the ideas and resources included in Chapter 7 as and when you need them, and remember that putting your personal life first is good for you professionally.

Ignore your feelings at your peril! Your emotions are there to protect and guide you through the trials and tribulations of life, and deserve your respect and your attention. Notice your own emotional patterns, and use Chapter 8 as a way of gaining a greater understanding of what is important to you. Simple strategies such as relaxation and exercise can make a huge difference to the control you have over your feelings. The taboo about seeking help from a counsellor or therapist is not what it once was, and there are other ways to get help in managing feelings, such as helplines and self-help books.

Stress can make you ill. Prolonged stress can make you very ill. Look at Chapter 9 to learn the warning signs, such as headaches and difficulty sleeping and, if you experience them, be warned! Start taking care of yourself by doing the little things that make a big difference, such as eating and drinking adequately and regularly. Try and get a sense of when you might get around to the bigger things, such as taking regular exercise or giving up smoking. Only you can decide when you are ready to make these changes, but if you put them off your old habits will take their toll on your health. Deciding to enjoy taking care of yourself makes the process a lot easier.

Finally, recognize that effective stress management is a lifelong commitment, but the commitment is to yourself and your future. If you want a happy, successful, healthy future, you will have no difficulty following the advice in this book. Develop a positive image of yourself as someone who is professional and can handle whatever the job throws at you, and you will be amazed to find the image becoming a reality!

Conclusion

So, what can you conclude from all of this? Well, firstly, that stress is serious and it is in your interests, as a teacher, to practise stress management. Not only will this help protect your health and enhance your quality of life, but also it will assist you in making progress in your career.

How do you accomplish this? As you can see from the summary above, managing stress is a complex business, involving many changes to your lifestyle, to the ways you interpret and manage your feelings and to the ways that you deal with people. Fortunately, many of these changes can be incorporated into your routine, and accomplishing them is more a matter of organization and self-discipline than expense or professional help. However, if your health is affected you are advised to discuss the problem with your doctor, who may be able to give you appropriate treatment. If you feel you do need more help, there are a number of resources available to help you including websites, self-help books, helplines and professionals such as counsellors and therapists. Details can be found throughout this book, and at Further resources, pages 149–55.

Finally, remember that stress management is not a 'one-off' event, but rather a lifelong process. In order to manage stress successfully, you need to make permanent changes to your behaviour. Fortunately, once you get into good habits it simply becomes a matter of maintenance, but it can be all too easy to fall back into the bad habits once exam marking comes around, or you experience a stressful life event. You owe it to yourself, your students and your loved ones to revisit the suggestions made in this book, and to evaluate and manage your stress on a regular basis. A stress-free life is a happy life!

FURTHER
RESOURCES

Teaching-specific resources

Assocation of Secondary Teachers Ireland (ASTI), ASTI House, Winetavern Street, Dublin 8, can be called on +353 1 6040160, and emailed at info@asti.ie. More information is available on their website at www.asti.ie.

Association of Teachers and Lecturers (ATL), 7 Northumberland Street, London, WC2N 5RD, can be called on 020 7930 6441, and emailed at info@atl.org.uk.

Department for Children, Schools and Families (DCSF): This new government department, previously the Department for Education and Skills (DfES), was set up on 28 June 2007. It can be accessed through their website at www.dfes.gov.uk.

Education and Inspection Act (2006) can be downloaded from the Office of Public Sector Information at http://www.opsi.gov.uk/ACTS/acts2006/20060040.htm and a timeline for the Act's implementation can be downloaded from teachernet at http://www.teachernet.gov.uk/educationandinspectionsacttimeline/

GMB (Britain's general union), Thorne House, 152 Brent Street, Hendon, London NW4 2DP, can be called on 020 8202 8272, and emailed at info@gmb.org.uk. Further details are available from their website at www.gmbunion.org.

Irish National Teacher's Organization (INTO), 35 Parnell Square, Dublin 1, can be called on +353 1 8047700, and emailed at info@into.ie. Further details are available on their website, at www.into.ie.

National Association of Headteachers (NAHT), 1 Heath Square, Boltro Road, Haywards Heath, West Sussex, RH16 1BL, can be called on 01444 472472, and emailed at info@naht.org.uk.

National Association of Schoolmasters Union of Women Teachers (NASUWT), headquarters can be called on 0121 453 6150, and emailed at nasuwt@mail.nasuwt.org.uk. They have many centres throughout the UK, which can be accessed through their website at www.nasuwt.org.uk.

National Healthy Schools Programme is a joint Department of Health and Department for Education and Skills initiative. It operates on a national, regional and local level. More details, including named contacts, are available from their website at www.healthyschools.gov.uk.

National Union of Teachers (NUT) headquarters, Hamilton House, Mabledon Place, London, WC1H 9BD, can be called on 020 7388 6191, and regional numbers and email addresses can be looked up on their website at www.teachers.org.uk.

Office for Standards in Education, Children's Services and Skills (Ofsted), Royal Exchange Buildings, St Ann's Square, Manchester, M2 7LA, can be called on 08456 404045, and emailed at enquiries@ofsted.gov.uk. Ofsted now carry out inspections in UK schools, childcare, further education and training, and all inspection reports are available on their website at www.ofsted.gov.uk, as well as updated details of the inspection process and publications and reports based on their findings.

Professional Association of Teachers (PAT) head office, 2 St James's Court, Friar Gate, Derby, DE1 1BT, can be called on 01332 372 337, and emailed at hp@pat.org.uk. Further details are available on their website at www.pat.org.uk.

Secondary Heads Association, 130 Regent Road, Leicester, LE1 7PG, can be called on 0116 299 1122, and emailed at info@sha.org.uk. Further details are available on their website at http://sha.eteach.com/page.asp.

Teacher Support Line provides 24-hour counselling for stressed teachers in England on 08000 562 561 and Wales on 08000 855 088, and for teachers in the Further and Higher Education sectors on 08000 32 99 52. You can also email from the website www.teachersupport.info.

Teacher Training Resource Bank (TTRB) provides access to the research and evidence base underpinning teacher education, and a range of other relevant materials. www.ttrb.ac.uk.

Teachernet has a database of over 2,000 teacher-approved lesson plans and resources that cover the National Curriculum Key Stages 1 to 3. http://www.teachernet.gov.uk/teachingand learning/resourcematerials/Resources/

Teachers' Union of Ireland (TUI), 73 Orwell Road, Rathgar, Dublin 6, Ireland can be called on +353 1 4922588, and can be emailed at tui@tui.ie. More details are available on their website at www.tui.ie.

Transport and General Workers' Union (TGWU), Transport House, 128 Theobalds Road, Holborn, London, WC1X 8TN, can be called on 020 7611 2500, and emailed at tgwu@tgwu.org.uk. Further details are available on their website at www.tgwu.org.uk.

Ulster Teachers' Union (UTU), 94 Malone Road, Belfast, BT9 5HP, can be called on 028 9066 2216, and emailed at office@utu.edu. More details are available on their website, at www.utu.edu.

UNISON, 1 Mabledon Place, London, WC1H 9AJ, can be called on 0845 355 0845. Contact details of their 12 regional offices can be found on their website at www.unison.org.uk.

University and College Union (UCU), 27 Britannia Street, London, WC1X 9JP, can be called on 020 7837 3636, and emailed at hq@ucu.org.uk. More details are available on their website, at www.ucu.org.uk.

Welsh Assembly Government, Department for Education, Life-long Learning and Skills can be called on 0845 010 3300, and emailed at DELLSWebTeam@wales.gsi.gov.uk. More details including office locations throughout Wales are available on their website at http://new.wales.gov.uk/topics/educationand skills/?lang=en.

Helplines

Advisory, Conciliation and Arbitration Service (ACAS) can provide information and advice on resolving disputes at work, including equality and diversity issues. Their lines are open from 8.00am–6.00pm: 08457 474747.

MALE helpline (Men's Advice Line and Enquiries) for men experiencing domestic violence, calls charged at local rate, Monday–Thursday, 10.00am–4.00pm: 0845 064 6800.

National Domestic Violence Helpline offers support and options from women supporters, free, 24-hour: 0808 2000 247.

Quitline provide help with quitting smoking, free, 9.00am–9.00pm every day except Christmas Day: 0800 00 22 00.

Samaritans offer emotional support, calls charged at local rate, 24-hour: In the UK dial 08457 90 90 90, in the Republic of Ireland dial 1850 60 90 90.

Saneline provides mental health support, calls charged at local rate, 12.00 noon until 2.00am every day: 0845 767 8000.

UK National Drugs helpline, free, 24-hour: 0800 77 66 00.

Websites

Affirmations. You can sign up to receive a daily affirmation via email at www.sunnythoughts.com.

Alcohol Concern have a searchable database of local alcohol services: www.alcoholconcern.org.uk.

Alcoholics Anonymous are a worldwide self-help support group for people with alcohol problems: www.alcoholics-anonymous.org.uk.

Author's website: www.drhartney.com.

British Association for Counselling and Psychotherapy (BACP), the regulatory body for counsellors and psychotherapists: www.bacp.co.uk.

British Psychological Society (BPS), the regulatory body for psychologists: www.bps.org.uk.

Cruse provide bereavement information and counselling: www.crusebereavementcare.org.uk.

Department of Health's website: www.dh.gov.uk.

Divorce Aid provide information on divorce: www.divorceaid.-co.uk.

Every Child Matters: Change for Children is a government initiative for children's needs and well-being. Teachers are responsible for, and build relationships with, their pupils and it is important that teachers are aware of the various services and initiatives to help them support children. More information is available on the website at www.everychildmatters.gov.uk.

Health and Safety Executive (HSE) can be called on 0845 345 0055. This is HSE's public enquiry contact centre, which provides access to workplace health and safety information, guidance and expert advice. More information is available on their website: www.hse.gov.uk.

Meditation Center offer information and guidelines on the practice of meditation: www.meditationcenter.com.

Narcotics Anonymous provides mutual support for people with serious addictions: www.ukna.org.

Parent Talk provide books, information, coaching and support to parents: www.parenttalk.org.uk

Quit provides help with stopping smoking: www.quit.org.uk.

Relate provide relationship and marriage counselling: www.re-late.org.uk.

Strengths and personality traits assessment using various online questionnaires: www.personalitystrengths.com.

VIA Inventory of Strengths allows you to assess your personal strengths and values: www.viastrengths.org.

Audio/video/DVD

Progressive Muscle Relaxation (PMR): Systematic approach to inducing relaxation by tensing and releasing muscle groups, in sequence, throughout the body. An audio recording of the author providing instructions in PMR is available for download at: www.drhartney.com.

4 Minute Fitness™: This approach uses dynamic principles from t'ai chi, yoga, meditation and ancient qi gong (chi kung), and combines them with modern medical theories, relaxation methods and key motivational techniques used by athletes, into an integrated four minute workout that has been shown by research to reduce teacher stress. Videos/DVDs can be ordered from: www.4minutefitness.com. The creator, Dr Keith Jefferey, will also travel anywhere in the world to run workshops, and may offer discounts. He can be emailed at kj@4MinuteFitness.com.

10-minute solution: This series of 10-minute DVD workouts are designed to fit into a busy lifestyle. They are taught by very competent instructors and include warm-ups, cool downs and stretching within the 10 minutes. Each DVD contains five workouts, each focused on a different body area or goal. A wide variety of types of exercise are available in the series, including kick-boxing, pilates, target toning, carb and calorie burner, dance and yoga. You can read about these on www.anchorbayentertainment.com/fitness. They are widely available in shops, but can also be ordered online through www.amazon.com.

Image and dress

Jackson, C. (1981) *Color Me Beautiful*, New York: Ballantine Books

Jackson, C. and Lulow, K. (1987) *Color For Men*, New York: Ballantine Books

Klein, B., Woodall, T. and Constantine, S. (2003) *Trinny And Susannah – The Rules (DVD)*, 2 Entertain Video

Kelly, C. and London, S. (2006) *Dress Your Best: Complete Guide to Finding the Style That Is Right for Your Body*, New York: Dell Publishing

Klein, B., Woodall, T. and Constantine, S. (2003) *Trinny And Susannah – The Rules (DVD)*, 2 Entertain Video

Woodall, T. and Constantine, S. (2002) *What Not to Wear*, London: Weidenfeld & Nicolson

Woodall, T. and Constantine, S. (2003) *What Not to Wear 2: For Every Occasion*, London: Weidenfeld & Nicolson

Woodall, T. and Constantine, S. (2004) *What You Wear Can Change Your Life*, London: Weidenfeld & Nicolson

Woodall, T. and Constantine, S. (2005) *What Your Clothes Say About You: How to Look Different, Act Different and Feel Different*, London: Weidenfeld & Nicolson

References

Adams, G., King, L. & King, D. (1996) 'Relationships of job and family involvement, family social support, and work-family conflict with job and life satisfaction', *Journal of Applied Psychology* 81, 411–20

Admiraal, W., Korthagen, F. & Wubbels, T. (2000) 'Effects of student teachers' coping behaviour', *British Journal of Educational Psychology*, 70(1), 33–52

Agervold, M. & Mikkelsen, E. (2004) 'Relationships between bullying, psychosocial work environment and individual stress reactions', *Work & Stress*, 18(4), 336–51

Al-Mohannadi, A. & Capel, S. (2007) 'Stress in physical education teachers in Qatar', *Social Psychology of Education*, 10(1), 55–75

Antoniou, A., Polychroni, F. & Vlachakis, A. (2006) 'Gender and age differences in occupational stress and professional burnout between primary and high-school teachers in Greece', *Journal of Managerial Psychology*, 21(7), 682–90

Ashforth, B. & Humphrey, R. (1995) 'Emotion in the workplace: a reappraisal', *Human Relations*, 48, 97–124

ATL, DfES, GMB, NAHT, NASUWT, NEOST, PAT, SHA, TGWU, UNISON and WAG (2003), *Raising standards and tackling workload: a national agreement*, Time for Standards (available online: http://www.tda.gov.uk/upload/resources/na_standards_workload.pdf)

Babyak, M., Blumenthal, J., Herman, S., Khatri, P., Doraiswamy, M., Moore, K., Craighead, W., Baldewicz, T. & Krishnan, K. (2000) 'Exercise treatment for major depression: maintenance of therapeutic benefit at 10 months', *Psychosomatic Medicine*, 62(5), 633–8

Bakker, A., Schaufeli, W., Demerouti, E., Janssen, P., Van Der Hulst, R. & Brouwer, J. (2000) 'Using equity theory to examine the difference between burnout and depression', *Anxiety, Stress, and Coping*, 13, 247–68

Ball, S. (2003) 'The teacher's soul and the terrors of performativity', *Journal of Education Policy*, 18(2), 215–28

Banks, J. & Gannon, L. (1988) 'The influence of hardiness on the relationship between stressors and psychosomatic symptomatology', *American Journal of Community Psychology*, 16, 25–37

Baucom, D. & Aiken, P. (1981) 'Effect of depressed mood on eating among obese and nonobese dieting and nondieting persons', *Journal of Personality and Social Psychology*, 41(3), 577–85

Berk, L., Felten, D., Tan, S., Bittman, B. & Westengard, J. (2001) 'Modulation of neuroimmune parameters during the eustress of humor-associated mirthful laughter', *Alternative Therapies in Health & Medicine*, 7(2), 62–72

Bernstein, A. (2001) *Emotional Vampires: Dealing With People Who Drain You Dry*, London: McGraw-Hill Professional

Bibou-Nakou, I., Stogiannidou, A. & Kiosseoglou, G. (1999) 'The relation between teacher burnout and teachers' attributions and practices regarding school behaviour problems', *School Psychology International*, 20(2), 209–17

Björkqvist, K. Österman, K. & Hjelt-Bäck, M. (1994) 'Aggression among university employees, *Aggressive Behavior*, 20(3), 173–84

Blix, A., Cruise, R., Mitchell, B. & Blix, G. (1994) 'Occupational stress among university teachers', *Educational Research*, 36(2), 157–69

Bond, F. & Bunce, D. (2000) 'Mediators of change in emotion-focused and problem-focused worksite stress management interventions', *Journal of Occupational Health Psychology*, 5(1), 156–63

Boyle, G., Borg, M., Falzon, J. & Baglioni, A. (1995) 'A structural model of the dimensions of teacher stress', *British Journal of Educational Psychology*, 65(1), 49–67

Brimblecombe, N. & Ormston, M. (1995) 'Teachers' perceptions of school inspection: A stressful experience', *Cambridge Journal of Education*, 25(1), 53–62

Brinkman, R. & Kirschner, R. (2002) *Dealing with Relatives (Even When You Can't Stand Them): Bringing Out the Best in Families at Their Worst*, London: McGraw-Hill Education

Brouwers, A. & Tomic, W. (2000) 'A longitudinal study of teacher burnout and perceived self-efficacy in classroom management', *Teaching and Teacher Education*, 16, 239–53

Brown, M., Ralph, S. & Brember, I. (2002) 'Change-linked work-related stress in British teachers', *Research in Education*, 67, 1–12

Cannon, W. B. (1932) *The wisdom of the body*, New York: Norton

Capel, S. (1997) 'Changes in students' anxieties and concerns after their first and second teaching practices', *Educational Research* 39, 211–28

Cavanaugh, M., Boswell, W., Roehling, M. & Boudreau, J. (2000) 'An empirical examination of self-reported work stress among US managers', *Journal of Applied Psychology*, 85(1), 65–74

Chan, D. & Hui, E. (1995) 'Burnout and coping among Chinese secondary school teachers in Hong Kong', *British Journal of Educational Psychology*, 65, 15–25

Chorney, L. (1998) 'Self-defeating beliefs and stress in teachers', *Dissertation Abstracts International Section A: Humanities and Social Sciences*, 58(10–A), 3830

Clayton, P. (2003) *Body language at work: read the signs and make the right moves*, London: Hamlyn

Cobb, S. & Rose, R. (1973) 'Hypertension, peptic ulcer and diabetes in air traffic controllers', *Journal of the American Medical Association*, 224, 489–92

Cohen, S., Tyrrell, D. & Smith, A. (1991) 'Psychological stress and susceptibility to the common cold', *New England Journal of Medicine*, 325, 606–12

Conner, M., Fitter, M. & Fletcher, W. (1999) 'Stress and snacking: a diary study of daily hassles and between-meal snacking', *Psychology and Health*, 14, 51–63

Cooper, C. & Cartwright, S. (2004) *Deal with stress: how to take control of your work*, London: Bloomsbury

Cooper, C. & Kelly, M. (1993) 'Occupational stress in head-teachers: a national UK study', *British Journal of Educational Psychology*, 63(1), 130–43

Cooper, C. & Sadri, G. (1991) 'The impact of stress counselling at work', *Journal of Social Behavior & Personality*, 6(7), 411–23

Davis, M., Robbins Eshelman, E. & McKay, M. (2000) *The relaxation and stress reduction workbook*, Oakland, CA: New Harbinger Publications

Delahanty, D., Herberman, H. & Craig, K. (1997) 'Acute and chronic distress and post-traumatic stress disorder as a function of responsibility for serious motor vehicle accidents', *Journal of Consulting and Clinical Psychology*, 65(4), 560–7

Dickson, A. (1982) *A woman in your own right*, London: Quartet

Douglas, M. (1996) 'Creating eustress in the workplace: a supervisor's role', *Supervision*, 57(10), 6–9

Edelmann, R. (1993) *Interpersonal conflicts at work*, Leicester: British Psychological Society

Elgin, S. (1990) *Staying well with the gentle art of verbal self-defense*, New York: MJF Books

Ferris, P. (2004) 'A preliminary typology of organizational response to allegations of workplace bullying: see no evil, hear no evil, speak no evil', *British Journal of Guidance & Counselling*, 32(3), 389–95

Firth-Cozens, J. & Hardy, G. (1992) 'Occupational stress, clinical treatment and changes in job perceptions', *Journal of Occupational & Organizational Psychology*, 65, 81–8

Forman, S. (1990) 'Rational-emotive therapy: contributions to teacher stress management', *School Psychology Review*, 19(3), 315–21

Frame, P. & Hartog, M. (2003) 'From rhetoric to reality. Into the swamp of ethical practice: implementing work-life balance', *Business Ethics: A European Review* 12(4), 358–68

Friedman, I. (2000a) 'Burnout in teachers: shattered dreams of impeccable professional performance', *Journal of Clinical Psychology*, 56, 595–606

Friedman, I. (2000b) 'Role pressures in school principals' work as predictors of burnout', *Megamot*, 40(2), 218–43

Frone, M., Russell, M. & Cooper, M. (1991) 'Relationship of work and family stressors to psychological distress: the independent moderating influence of social support, mastery, affective coping and self-focused attention', *Journal of Social Behavior & Personality*, 6, 227–50

Fuller, G. (2007) *Stress causes half of UK teachers to think about quitting*, PersonnelToday.com

Gmelch, W. (1983) 'Stress for success: how to optimise your performance', *Theory into Practice*, 22(1), 7–14

Goleman, D. (1996) *Emotional intelligence: why it can matter more than IQ*, London: Bloomsbury

Goodson, I. & Mangan, J. (1995) 'Subject cultures and the introduction of classroom computers', *British Educational Research Journal*, 21(5), 613–28

Grandjean, D., Sander, D., Pourtois, G., Schwartz, S., Seghier, M., Schere, K. & Vuilleumier, P. (2005) 'The voices of wrath: brain responses to angry prosody in meaningless speech', *Nature Neuroscience*, 8, 145–6

Griva, K. & Joekes, K. (2003) 'UK teachers under stress: can we predict wellness on the basis of the teaching job?', *Psychology and Health*, 18(4), 457–71

Hall, E., Hall, C. & Abaci, R. (1997) 'The effects of human relations training on reported teacher stress, pupil control ideology and locus of control', *British Journal of Educational Psychology*, 67(4), 483–96

Hart, P., Wearing, A. & Conn, M. (1995) 'Conventional wisdom is a poor predictor of the relationship between discipline policy, student misbehaviour and teacher stress', *British Journal of Educational Psychology*, 65(1), 27–48

Hartney, E. (2006) *How to manage stress in FE*, London: Continuum

Hartney, E. (2007) 'Strategies for the management of lecturer stress in feedback tutorials', *Active Learning in Higher Education*, 8(1), 99–116

Hartney, E., Orford, J., Dalton, S., Ferrins-Brown, M., Kerr, C. & Maslin, J. (2003) 'Untreated heavy drinkers: a qualitative and quantitative study of dependence and readiness to change', *Addiction Research & Theory*, 11(5), 317–37

Health and Safety Executive (2003) *Real solutions, real people: a managers' guide to tackling work-related stress*, Sudbury: HSE Books

Held, V. (1996) *How not to take it personally*, Whitby, ON: McGraw-Hill Ryerson

Heron, R., McKeown, S., Tomenson, J. & Teasdale, E. (1999) 'Study to evaluate the effectiveness of stress management workshops on response to general and occupational measures of stress', *Occupational Medicine*, 49(7), 451–7

Hickling, E., Blanchard, E., Buckley, T. & Taylor, A. (1999) 'Effects of attribution of responsibility for motor vehicle accidents on severity of PTSD symptoms, ways of coping, and recovery over six months', *Journal of Traumatic Stress*, 12(2), 345–53

Hiroto, D. & Seligman, M. (1975) 'Generality of learned helplessness in man', *Journal of Personality and Social Psychology*, 31, 311–27

Hobson, C., Delunas, L. & Kesic, D. (2001) 'Compelling evidence of the need for corporate work/life balance initiatives: results from a national survey of stressful life-events', *Journal of Employment Counseling*, 38(1), 38–44

Holmes, T. H. & Rahe, R. H. (1967) 'The social readjustment rating scale', *Journal of Psychosomatic Research*, 11(2), 213–18

Huang, X. & Liu, M. (2007) 'An analysis of the relationships between teacher efficacy, teacher self-esteem and orientations to seeking help', *Social Behaviour and Personality*, 35(5), 707–16

Hui, E. & Chan, D. (1996) 'Teacher stress and guidance work in Hong Kong secondary school teachers', *British Journal of Guidance & Counselling*, 24(2), 199–212

Jackson, A. (1993) *Stress Control through Self-Hypnosis*, London: Piatkus

Jacobsson, C., Pousette, A. & Thylefors, I. (2001) 'Managing stress and feelings of mastery among Swedish comprehensive school teachers', *Scandinavian Journal of Educational Research*, 45(1), 37–53

Jarvis, M. (2002) 'Teacher stress: a critical review of recent findings and suggestions for future', *Stress News*, 14(1), 1–6

Jeffers, S. (1987) *Feel the Fear and Do It Anyway*, New York: Random House

Jefferey, K. (2002) *4 Minute Fitness™: an Effective Stress Management Technique for Teachers*, unpublished dissertation for the Master's Degree in Education at the University of Victoria

Jex, S. & Eleacqua, T. (1999) 'Time management as a moderator of relations between stressors and employee strain', *Work & Stress*, 13(2), 182–91

Jones, F. & Bright, J. (2001) *Stress: Myth, Theory and Research*, Harlow: Pearson

Joseph, S. & Linley, P. (2005) 'Positive adjustment to threatening events: an organismic valuing theory of growth through adversity', *Review of General Psychology*, 9(3), 262–80

Judd, J. (1999) 'First teacher paid compensation for classroom stress', *Independent* (London), 1 October 1999

Judge, T. & Locke, E. (1993) 'Effects of dysfunctional thought processes on subjective well-being and job satisfaction', *Journal of Applied Psychology*, 78, 475–90

Juhasz, A. (1990) 'Teacher self-esteem: a triple-role approach to this forgotten dimension', *Education*, 111(2), 234–41

Karasek, R. (1990) 'Lower health risk with increased job control among white-collar workers', *Journal of Organisational Behavior*, 11, 171–85

Karasek, R., Baker, D., Marxer, F., Ahlbom, A. & Theorell, R. (1981) 'Job decision latitude, job demands and cardiovascular disease: a prospective study of Swedish men', *American Journal of Public Health*, 71, 694–705

Kiecolt-Glaser, J. and Glaser, R. (1995) 'Psychoneuroimmunology and health consequences: data and shared mechanisms', *Psychosomatic Medicine*, 57, 269–74

Kinman, G. & Jones, F. (2001) 'The home–work interface' in F. Jones & J. Bright (eds) *Stress: Myth, Theory and Research*, Harlow: Pearson, 199–220

Kivimäki, M., Leino-Arjas, P., Luukkonen, R., Riihimäki, H., Vahtera, J. & Kirjonen, J. (2002) 'Work stress and risk of cardiovascular mortality: prospective cohort study of industrial employees', *British Medical Journal*, 325, 857–60

Klusmann, U., Kunter, M. & Trautwein, U. (2006) 'Lehrerbelastung und Unterrichtsqualität aus der Perspektive von Lehrenden und Lernenden' [translated title: 'Teachers' stress and the quality of instruction: linking teachers' and students' perception'], *Zeitschrift für Pädagogische Psychologie/German Journal of Educational Psychology*, 20(3), 161–73

Ko, Y., Chan, K., Lai, G. & Boey, K. (2000) 'Stress and coping of

Singapore teachers: a quantitative and qualitative analysis', *Journal of Developing Societies*, 16(2), 181–200

Kobasa, S. (1979) 'Stressful life events, personality and health: an inquiry into hardiness', *Journal of Personality and Social Psychology*, 37, 1–11

Kremenitzer, J. (2005) 'The emotionally intelligent early childhood educator: self-reflective journaling', *Early Childhood Education Journal*, 33(1), 3–9

Kyriacou, C. (2001) 'Teacher stress: directions for future research', *Educational Review*, 53(1), 27–35

Laudenslager, M., Ryan, S., Drugan, R., Hyson, R. & Maier, S. (1983) 'Coping and immunosuppression: inescapable but not escapable shock suppresses lymphocyte proliferation', *Science*, 221, 568–70

Lazarus, R. & Folkman, S. (1984) *Stress, Appraisal and Coping*, New York: Springer

Le Fevre, M., Kolt, G. & Matheny, J. (2006) 'Eustress, distress and their interpretation in primary and secondary occupational stress management interventions: which way first?', *Journal of Managerial Psychology*, 21(6), 547–65

Lewis, D. (1999) 'Workplace bullying: interim findings of a study in further and higher education in Wales', *International Journal of Manpower*, 20(1/2), 106–18

Lewis, R. (1999) 'Teachers coping with the stress of classroom discipline', *Social Psychology of Education* 3, 155–71

Lusa, S., Häkkänen, M., Luukkonen, R. & Viikari-Juntura, E. (2002) 'Perceived physical work capacity, stress, sleep disturbance and occupational accidents among firefighters working during a strike', *Work & Stress* 16(3), 264–74

Lynch J., Krause, M., Kaplan, G., Tuomilehto, J. & Salonen, J. (1997) 'Workplace demands, economic reward and progression on carotid atherosclerosis', *Circulation*, 96, 302–7

Macan, T. (1994) 'Time management: test of a process model', *Journal of Applied Psychology*, 79(3), 381–91

Macan, T., Shahani, C., Dipboye, R. & Phillips, A. (1990) 'College students' time management: correlations with academic performance and stress', *Journal of Educational Psychology*, 82, 760–8

Marucha, P., Kiecolt-Glaser, J.K. & Favagehi, M. (1998) 'Mucosal wound healing is impaired by examination stress', *Psychosomatic Medicine*, 60, 362–5

Maslach, C., Schaufeli, W. & Leiter, M. (2001) 'Job burnout', *Annual Review of Psychology*, 52(1), 397–422

Mearns, J. & Cain, J. (2003) 'Relationships between teachers' occupational stress and their burnout and distress: roles of coping and negative mood regulation expectancies', *Anxiety, Stress and Coping*, 16(1), 71–82

Metcalfe, C., Smith, G., Wadsworth, E., Sterne, J., Heslop, P., Macleod, J. & Smith, A. (2003) 'A contemporary validation of the Reeder Stress Inventory', *British Journal of Health Psychology*, 8, 83–94

Michie, S. (1992) 'Evaluation of a stress management service', *Health Manpower Management* 18(1), 15–17

Michie, S. (1996) 'Reducing absenteeism by stress management: evaluation of stress counselling service', *Work & Stress*, 10(4), 367–72

Miller, G. & Travers, C. (2005) 'Ethnicity and the experience of work: job stress and satisfaction of minority ethnic teachers in the UK', *International Review of Psychiatry*, 17(5), 317–27

Moriarty, V., Edmonds, S., Blatchford, P. & Martin, C. (2001) 'Teaching young children: perceived satisfaction and stress', *Educational Research*, 43(1), 33–46

Morton, L., Vesco, R., Williams, N. & Awender, M. (1997) 'Student teacher anxieties related to class management, pedagogy, evaluation and staff relations', *British Journal of Educational Psychology*, 67, 69–89

National Association of Headteachers (2000), *Bullying*, Professional Management Series PM038, Sussex: NAHT (available online: http://www.naht.org.uk/userfiles/448805633/bullying.pdf)

National Education Association (2006) 'Relieving teacher stress', *Works 4 Me* [email newsletter]. Available online: http://www.nea.org/works4me/wm060517.html

National Union of Teachers (1999) *Tackling Stress*, NUT Health and Safety Briefing

Office of National Statistics (2004) *Online* (available online: www.statistics.gov.uk)

Ofsted (2005) *Healthy Minds: Promoting Emotional Health and Well-Being in Schools*, Ref: HMI 2457, London: Ofsted (available online: www.ofsted.gov.uk)

Ofsted (2006) *Improving Behaviour: Lessons learned from HMI monitoring of secondary schools where behaviour had been judged unsatisfactory*, Ref: HMI 2377, London: Ofsted (available online: www.ofsted.gov.uk)

Orford, J., Dalton, S., Hartney, E., Ferrins-Brown, M., Kerr, C. & Maslin, J. (2002a) 'How is excessive drinking maintained? Untreated heavy drinkers' experiences of the personal benefits and drawbacks of their drinking', *Addiction Research and Theory*, 10(4), 347–72

Orford, J., Dalton, S., Hartney, E., Ferrins-Brown, M., Kerr, C. & Maslin, J. (2002b) 'The close relatives of untreated heavy drinkers: perspectives on heavy drinking and its effects', *Addiction Research and Theory*, 10(5), 439–63

Parkes, K., Styles, E. & Broadbent, D. (1990) 'Work preferences as moderators of the effects of paced and unpaced work on mood and cognitive performance: a laboratory simulation of mechanized letter sorting', *Human Factors*, 32, 197–216

Pearson, L. & Moomaw, W. (2005) 'The relationship between teacher autonomy and stress, work satisfaction, empowerment, and professionalism', *Educational Research Quarterly*, 29(1), 37–53

Pithers, R. & Soden, R. (1998) 'Scottish and Australian teacher stress and strain: a comparative study', *British Journal Of Educational Psychology*, 68(2), 269–79

PricewaterhouseCoopers (2001), *Teacher Workload Study: Interim Report*, A Review commissioned by Department for Education and Skills (DfES)

Ray, D. (2007) 'Two counseling interventions to reduce teacher-child relationship stress', *Professional School Counseling*, 10(4), 428–40

Reed, G., Kemeny, M., Taylor, S. & Visscher, B. (1999) 'Negative HIV-specific expectancies and AIDS–related bereavement as predictors of symptom onset in asymptomatic HIV-positive gay men', *Health Psychology*, 18, 354–63

Rees, S. & Graham, R. (1991) *Assertion Training: How to Be Who You Really Are*, London: Routledge

Reynolds, S., Taylor, E. & Shapiro, D. (1993) 'Session impact and outcome in stress management training', *Journal of Community & Applied Social Psychology*, 3, 325–37

Ritvanen, T., Louhevaara, V., Helin, P., Väisänen, S. & Hänninen, O. (2006) 'Responses of the autonomic nervous system during periods of perceived high and low work stress in younger and older female teachers', *Applied Ergonomics*, 37(3), 311–18

Rubin, T. (1997) *The angry book*, New York: Simon & Schuster

Rydstedt, L., Devereux, J. & Furnham, A. (2004) 'Are lay theories of work stress related to distress? A longitudinal study in the British workforce', *Work & Stress*, 18(3), 245–54

Salmela-Aro, K., Näätänen, P. & Nurmi, J. (2004) 'The role of work-related personal projects during two burnout interventions: a longitudinal study', *Work & Stress*, 18(3), 208–30

Sapolsky, R. (2004) *Why zebras don't get ulcers* (3rd edn), New York: Henry Holt

Searle, B., Bright, J. & Bochner, S. (1999) 'Testing the three-factor model of occupational stress: the impacts of demands, control and social support on a mail sorting task', *Work & Stress*, 13, 268–79

Selye, H. (1956) *The stress of life*, New York: McGraw-Hill

Sheehan, M. (1999) 'Workplace bullying: responding with some emotional intelligence', *International Journal of Manpower*, 20(1/2), 57–69

Sheffield, D., Dobbie, D. & Carroll, D. (1994) 'Stress, social support and psychological and physical wellbeing in secondary school teachers', *Work & Stress*, 8, 235–43

Shimahara, N. & Sakai, A. (1992) 'Teacher internship and the culture of teaching in Japan', *British Journal of Sociology of Education*, 13(2), 147–62

Simmons, B. & Nelson, D. (2001) 'Eustress at work: the relationship between hope and health in hospital nurses', *Health Care Management Review*, 26(4), 7–18

Smith, J. (2004) *The Bloke's Guide to Pregnancy*, London: Hay House

Smith, K. & Milstein, M. (1984) 'Stress and teachers: old wine in new bottles', *Urban Education*, 19(1), 39–51

Solomon, G., Temoshok, L., O'Leary, A. & Zich, J. (1987) 'An intensive psychoimmunologic study of long-surviving persons with AIDS: pilot work background studies, hypotheses, and methods', *Annals New York Academy of Sciences*, 46, 647–55

Sparks, K., Faragher, B. & Cooper, C. (2001) 'Well being and occupational health in the 21st century workplace', *Journal of Occupational & Organizational Psychology*, 74, 489–509

Steiner, C. (1981) *The other side of power*, New York: Grove Press

Stoppard, M. (2004) *Conception, Pregnancy and Birth*, London: Dorling Kindersley

Stough, L. & Emmer, E. (1998) 'Teachers' emotions and test feedback', *International Journal of Qualitative Studies in Education*, 11(2), 341–61

Street, P. (2007) 'What a performance: recognizing performing arts skills in the delivery of lectures in higher education', *The Learning Teacher Journal* 1(1), 3–22

Stubbs, D. (1985) *Assertiveness at Work*, London: Pan Books

Taris, T., Van Horn, J., Schaufeli, W. & Schreurs, P. (2004) 'Inequity, burnout and psychological withdrawal among teachers: a dynamic exchange model', *Anxiety, Stress & Coping*, 17(1), 103–22

Teacher Support Network (2006) *The National Agreement on cutting teacher workload and what it means for classroom teachers*, Teacher Support Network (available online at www.teacher-support.info)

Teasdale, E., Heron, R. & Tomenson, J. (2000) 'Bringing health to life' in L. Murphy & C. Cooper (eds) *Healthy and Productive Work: An International Perspective*, London: Taylor & Francis

Travers, C. & Cooper, C. (1993) 'Mental health, job satisfaction and occupational stress among UK teachers', *Work and Stress*, 7(3), 203–19

Travers, C. & Cooper, C. (1996) *Teachers Under Pressure: Stress in the Teaching Profession*, London: Routledge

Travers, C. & Cooper, C. (1997) 'Stress in teaching' in D. Shorrocks-Taylor, (ed.) *Directions in educational psychology*, London: Whurr

Trendall, C. (1989) 'Stress in teaching and teacher effectiveness: a study of teachers across mainstream and special education', *Educational Research*, 31(1), 52–8

Van der Lindl, C. (2001) 'The teacher's stress and its implications for the school as an organization: how can TQM help?', *Education*, 121(2), 375–82

Van Horn, J., Schaufeli, W. & Enzmann, D. (1999) 'Teacher burnout and lack of reciprocity', *Journal of Applied Social Psychology*, 29, 91–108

Van Horn, J., Schaufeli, W. & Taris, T. (2001) 'Lack of reciprocity among Dutch teachers: validation of reciprocity indices and their relationship to stress and well-being', *Work and Stress*, 15(3), 191–213

Wade, A. & Dyer, C. (2003) 'Even when she was being nice I felt terrified', *Guardian*, 25 November 2003

Wang, W. & Guo, L. (2007) 'An investigation on occupational stress, teacher burnout and mental health state of primary and middle schools teachers and the relations among them', *Chinese Journal of Clinical Psychology*, 15(2), 146–48

Watts, W. & Short, A. (1990) 'Teacher drug use: a response to occupational stress', *Journal of Drug Education*, 20(1), 47–65

Westman, M. (1990) 'The relationship between stress and performance: the moderating effect of hardiness', *Human Performance*, 3(3), 141–55

Whatmore, L., Cartwright, S. & Cooper, C. (1999) 'United Kingdom: evaluation of a stress management programme in the public sector' in M. Kompier & C. Cooper (eds) *Preventing Stress, Improving Productivity: European Case Studies in the Workplace*, London: Routledge

Widdowson, R. (2003) *Yoga for pregnancy*, London: Hamlyn

Yoon, J. (2002) 'Teacher characteristics as predictors of teacher-student relationships: stress, negative affect and self-efficacy', *Social Behavior and Personality*, 30(5), 485–494

Index

accomplishment 12, 26, 35, 54, 56, 75, 135, 142
accountability 41
action plan 24, 39, 52, 53, 142, 144
activity 9, 27,114, 120
acupuncture 135–7
acute 3, 129–31, 144
adapt 6, 18, 54, 108
adaptation 71
adaptive 119
administrator 11, 63
advice 2, 3, 4, 23, 31, 32, 39, 41, 85, 113, 126, 127, 134, 141, 143, 144, 146, 149–55, 169
AIDS *see* human immunodeficiency virus disease
alcohol 10, 13, 126, 133–4, 152
allergies 129
anger 3, 18, 76, 91, 117–18, 119, 127, 143
antidepressant 121
appraisal 7
arousal 6, 14
assumptions 102
attentional disorder 83
attitude 29, 57, 80, 98, 135, 136, 144
    cynical 54
    optimistic 16

positive 24–7, 60, 144
awareness 78, 101, 111, 127, 141

balancing
    professional and personal life 3, 103–14, 143, 146
    unequal relationships 86
behaviour
    acceptable 51, 83, 118 *see also* behaviour, appropriate
    aggressive 3, 85, 90–6, 143, 145
    altering 87
    appropriate 83, 95 *see also* behaviour, acceptable
    assertive 3, 87, 90–3, 101, 143, 145
    bad 80, 88, 95 *see also* behaviour, negative
    bullying *see* bullying
    condescending 81
    difficult 86
    disrespectful 76, 80
    expected 83
    good 96 *see also* behaviour, positive
    inappropriate 87, 88
    indirect 3, 75, 87, 90–4, 95, 98, 143, 145
    passive 3, 52, 86, 87, 90–4, 98, 123, 143, 145

and personalities 3, 90, 101, 143, 145

positive 46 *see also* behaviour, good

time management *see* time management

unhealthy 10, 114

unreasonable 111

behavioural difficulties 83–4

bereavement 3, 112, 143

biofeedback 136–7

body language 87, 88, 102

body scan 28

boredom 17

bossy people 3, 96–7

boundaries 105–6

brainstorm 19

breathing 27–9, 40, 132

bullying 3, 12, 21, 37, 76, 81, 82, 83, 84–8

burnout 11–12, 14, 16–17, 36, 39–41, 47, 54, 56, 75, 76, 78, 85, 86, 87, 116, 142, 144

caffeine 10, 13, 22, 133–4

cancer 10, 129

care 4, 21, 25, 44, 56, 62, 69, 90, 98, 100, 101, 129, 130, 135, 146

career 2, 6, 14, 24, 47–8, 59, 61–72, 104, 133, 142, 143, 145, 147

childbirth 3, 109–11, 143

childcare 3, 42, 65, 109–11, 143

children 21, 41, 42, 50, 56, 62, 79, 104, 109, 111, 146, 149, 153

chronic 3, 13, 76, 129–31, 132, 135, 144

cigarettes 13, 131, 133–4 *see also* nicotine

coaching 3, 36, 52, 102, 113, 123–5, 153

college 65, 66, 151

commitment 16, 46. 68, 125, 127, 146

common cold 10

communication 12, 38, 52, 74, 85, 90–94, 95, 96, 98, 100, 101, 111, 140

skills 24, 37–9, 144

community 46, 114

competence 12, 21, 55, 62, 75, 85, 87, 90

competitiveness 41, 79, 81

complain 19

complaining 13, 78

complaint 45, 81, 86, 136

complementary therapies 4, 136–7 144

conflict 30, 38, 39, 74, 77, 78, 84, 85, 92

coping 3, 9, 16, 36, 52, 78, 102, 109, 112–13, 122, 125, 143

coronary heart disease 10

counselling 3, 36, 77, 102, 112, 122–3, 125, 126, 127, 143, 150, 152, 153

counsellor 23, 52, 101, 102, 120, 122, 123, 125, 126, 127, 146 *see also* psychotherapist

creativity 17, 41

credibility 136

cultural 7, 41, 105, 106

culture 7, 26, 39, 41–4, 48, 70, 78, 87, 91, 114, 134, 144

damage 9, 10, 81, 112, 123

day-job teacher 66–7

definitions 2, 6–7, 142

dependency 13, 80

dependent 71, 111, 126

depersonalization 11, 54, 56, 75
depression 11, 71, 76, 86, 93, 102, 120
diet 10, 109, 135, 139
difficult people 2, 3, 32, 89–102, 143, 145
disability 26, 77, 83, 129, 135
disabled 83
disease 9–10, 129–31 *see also* illness
disinterest 110
distress 18, 22, 25, 116 *see also* negative stress
divorce 3, 111–12, 143, 146, 153
dizziness 11
doctor 23, 35, 102, 110, 120, 121, 131, 132, 133, 135, 136, 147 *see also* general practitioner
drugs 113, 133–4, 137, 152

emotion 3, 115–27
emotional 6, 11, 12, 13, 19, 24, 34, 37, 39, 46, 102, 105, 107, 109, 112, 116, 121, 136
    exhaustion 11, 56, 75, 142, 146, 152
    intelligence 37
energy 2, 11, 20, 35, 70, 71, 82, 109, 117, 118, 121, 134, 135, 137, 143, 145
environment 3, 14, 24, 28, 40, 47, 54, 55, 80, 101, 116, 118
envy 79, 81, 99, 110
equity theory 76
eustress 18–19, 22, 25, 26, 47 *see also* positive stress
exercise 9, 10, 22, 24, 27, 34–6, 46, 47, 121, 135, 144, 146, 154
exhausted 12, 54, 67, 109 *see also* exhaustion

exhaustion 11, 12, 13, 17, 56, 75, 142 *see also* exhausted

fabrication 58
failure versus feedback 3, 70–1
fall-back teacher 65–6,
family problems 79, 112–13
fatigue 13, 17, 110 *see also* tiredness
favouritism 64, 79
fear 3, 18, 42, 44, 59, 99, 108, 113, 117, 119–20, 135, 143
feedback 3, 52, 53, 58, 59, 60, 70, 71, 77, 87, 90, 97, 102, 123, 143, 145
female 57, 81, 141 *see also* women
fight or flight 6, 40, 117, 119
financial 12, 104, 105, 109, 112, 123
flattery 93, 94
flexibility 65
friendships 113, 114

general practitioner 20, 123, 136 *see also* doctor
goals 2, 19, 33, 41, 46, 48, 55, 56, 69, 108, 123, 143, 145 *see also* targets
GP *see* general practitioner
guilt 41, 53, 92, 93, 100

habits 3, 28, 132, 144, 146, 147
harassment ix,12, 21, 81–88
hardiness 16
hardy *see* hardiness
hassles 16
headaches 11, 22, 129, 131, 132, 134, 146
health
    mental 2, 11, 46, 142, 152
    physical ix, 9–10, 113

problems ix, 3, 46, 129–31, 144
health-promoting 132–33
heart 10, 11, 40, 97
heartless 101
helplessness 12 *see also* learned
    helplessness
helplines 3, 112, 113, 122, 126–7,
    134, 143, 146, 147, 151–2
HIV *see* human immunodeficiency
    virus disease
home 12, 21, 27, 66, 83, 100, 104,
    106, 107, 114, 145, 146
hope 22, 23, 25, 27, 107, 134, 140
hopeless 19
hopelessness 12
human immunodeficiency virus
    disease 10, 129
humour 18, 22, 23, 25, 27, 82, 119
    see also eustress
hypertension 10
hypnosis *see* self hypnosis

IBS *see* irritable bowel syndrome
identity 13, 50, 53–6, 104, 142
illness 13, 17, 59, 101, 104, 112,
    129, 130, 135
insomnia 27
invincible 13
irritable bowel syndrome 129

judgement 7, 12, 45, 59, 91, 92

lazy people 95, 98, 99, 100, 104,
    143, 145
learned helplessness 71, 91–2
learning disability 26
life events 16, 108, 146, 161

male 57, 141 *see also* men *see also*
    Men's Advice Line and
    Enquiries (MALE)

manager 39, 44–7, 48, 63–4, 82,
    86, 87, 144
manager-in-training 63–4
manipulative people 3, 98–100
marriage 3, 108, 111, 143, 146,
    153
massage 136–7
medication 13, 22, 121
men 57, 66, 81, 104, 109, 111,
    141, 152 *see also* male
Men's Advice Line and Enquiries
    (MALE) 113, 152
mentoring 3, 123–5, 126
mind-reading 38
mistakes 14, 96
mood 35, 37, 100, 101, 110, 113,
    121 *see also* moody people
moody people 3, 100–1 *see also*
    mood
motivation 2, 19–20, 21, 50, 65,
    71, 117

National Agreement 27, 30–2, 41,
    42, 45, 78, 81, 82, 106, 111
National Healthy Schools
    Programme 46
National Healthy Schools
    Standards (NHSS) *see* National
    Healthy Schools Programme
negative stress 18–19, 25, 36, 47,
    54 *see also* distress
negotiating 38
nicotine 13, 133 *see also* cigarettes

Office for Standards in Education
    41, 46, 56–60, 64, 83, 150
OFSTED *see* Office for Standards in
    Education

pain 13, 24, 113, 116, 121, 131,
    132

painkillers 22, 34, 132, 136
PANDA report *see* Performance
and Assessment Report
PAT *see* Pupil Achievement
Tracker
perceptions 8, 14, 18, 53, 57, 64
performance 41, 55, 58, 64, 71,
119, 123
Performance and Assessment
Report 58
performativity 41, 42
performing *see* performance
personal relationships 3, 103–14,
146
personality 3, 21, 34, 69, 84, 85,
87, 89–102, 122, 143, 153
personality *see* behaviour, and
personalities, *see also* moody
people, *see also* bossy people, *see
also* manipulative people, *see
also* lazy people
planning 2, 8, 20, 32, 34, 55, 78,
110, 127, 135
pleasure 18, 20, 63, 131 *see also*
eustress
PMR *see* progressive muscle
relaxation
policy 51, 52, 83, 86, 88, 145
positive stress 18, 19, 22, 23, 25,
27, 47 *see also* eustress
post-traumatic stress disorder 131
power plays 3, 81–4, 87, 143,
145
praise 53, 79, 96
pregnancy 3, 109–11, 143
pressure 6, 16, 25, 30, 43, 75, 110,
137, 139
productive 87
productivity 106
profession 8, 41, 54, 55, 62, 66,
124

professional 2, 3, 8, 20, 26, 31, 32,
40, 41, 42, 43, 45, 47, 55, 57,
62, 66, 68, 85, 102, 103–14,
116, 120, 121, 122, 123, 124,
136, 143, 144, 145, 146, 147,
150
image 4, 140–2, 144
teacher 62–3, 66, 140
professionalism 54, 63, 19
progressive muscle relaxation 29,
144, 154
psychotherapist 122–3 *see also*
counsellor
psychotherapy 3, 36, 102, 122–3,
143, 152
PTSD *see* post-traumatic stress
disorder
Pupil Achievement Tracker 58

quality of life 2, 9, 12–14, 135,
139, 142, 147

racial 87, 88
RAISEonline *see* Reporting and
Analysis for Improvement
through School Self-
Evaluation
reciprocity 3, 74, 76, 94, 143
Reporting and Analysis for
Improvement through School
Self-Evaluation 58
reflexology 137
relationship rules 3, 77–80, 82,
143, 145
relationships 73–88, 96, 103–14,
142, 143, 146, 153
with colleagues 73–88, 145
with students 73–88
relax 13, 28, 29, 34, 40, 108, 132,
133 *see also* relaxation, *see also*
relaxation skills

relaxation 27–30, 46, 47, 60, 110,
   118, 119, 132, 135, 144, 146,
   154 *see also* relax, *see also*
   relaxation skills
   skills 9, 29, 47, 60 *see also* relax,
      see also relaxation
resources 8, 11, 24, 30, 33, 87,
   107, 134, 146, 147, 148–55
respond 6, 7, 8, 19, 20, 37, 52, 75,
   80, 82, 94, 101, 145
response 6, 8, 18, 28, 34, 40, 77,
   82, 86, 94, 97, 101, 117, 119,
   130
rest 110, 131, 135
restful 13, 134
rheumatoid arthritis 129
rustout 16–17, 39–41, 47, 98, 144

sadness 3, 120–1, 143
satisfaction 17, 18, 19, 30, 40, 54,
   57, 71, 74
scared *see* fear
school 8, 17, 21, 25, 26, 28, 31, 32,
   33, 40, 42, 43, 45, 46, 47, 51,
   56, 57, 58, 59, 60, 62, 63, 64,
   65, 66, 67, 68, 83, 106, 111,
   117, 123, 137, 140, 145, 156,
   157
secrecy 93
security 8
SEF *see* Self Evaluation Form
self-control 30
self-discipline 80, 127, 147
self-esteem 13, 17, 55, 56, 87, 161
Self Evaluation Form 58
self-help
   books 9, 102, 127, 143, 146,
      147
   groups 3, 9, 102, 122, 125–6,
      134, 143
self-hypnosis 30, 144

self-image 2, 13, 53–6, 142
self-promotion 3, 70, 143, 145
self-reflection 69, 145
sleep 12, 13, 20, 34, 93, 102, 132,
   133, 134, 135 *see also* sleeping
sleeping 10, 22, 110, 131, 132, 146
   see also sleep
sleeping pills 22
socializing 113
squeamishness 110
status 45, 53, 56, 74
strengths 52–3, 58, 69, 102, 153
stress test 20–3, 144
stress-management skills 24,
   27–36, 46, 71, 144
suffering 11, 12, 43, 44, 102, 130
support staff 27, 32, 45, 78, 81, 82,
   140
survival 116
survive 6, 42
symptoms 11, 17, 24, 26, 36, 54,
   56, 75, 78, 85, 102, 109, 129,
   131, 132, 134, 144

targets 2, 41, 43 *see also* goals
techniques 4, 6, 23, 36, 83, 86, 88,
   111, 122, 142, 144, 154
therapist 125, 136, 146, 147
   hypno- 30,
   psycho- 122–3, 152
threat 6, 13, 18, 26, 45, 81, 84, 85,
   87, 88, 99, 119
time management 9, 27, 30, 32,
   33, 47, 144
tiredness 13, 131, 132 *see also*
   fatigue
trade union 12, 17, 32, 36, 45, 53,
   60, 97, 149–51
trauma 137
treatment 4, 102, 121, 125, 135–7,
   144, 147

trust 50, 108, 119

undefined career teacher 67–8
unhappiness 12, 43, 116 *see also*
    sadness
union *see* trade union
university 26, 66, 68, 151

values 41, 55, 57, 69, 153
vanity 99
victim 13, 20, 34, 82, 85, 86, 99,
    135
violence 87, 88, 112, 152
vulnerable 54, 101

warning signs 3, 131, 132, 144,
    146
weak 13
weakness 45, 69

witness 82
women 58, 81, 93, 104, 109, 111,
    141, 149, 152 *see also*
    female
workplace 41, 43, 78, 82, 107,
    108, 116
    bullying 37, 84–8 *see also*
        bullying
    culture 39, 41, 42–4, 48, 87,
        144
    disputes 110
    health and safety 153
    relationships 143
    stress 9, 27, 42–4
    toxic 95
worry 8, 20, 29, 58, 83, 94, 101,
    107, 110, 119, 135
worrying *see* worry
wound healing 10